COLLEGE FOR STUDENTS WITH DISABILITIES

of related interest

**Supporting College and University Students
with Invisible Disabilities**
A Guide for Faculty and Staff Working with Students with Autism,
AD/HD, Language Processing Disorders, Anxiety, and Mental Illness
Christy Oslund
ISBN 978 1 84905 955 8
eISBN 978 0 85700 785 8

Succeeding in College with Asperger Syndrome
A Student Guide
John Harpur, Maria Lawlor and Michael Fitzgerald
ISBN 978 1 84310 201 4
eISBN 978 1 84642 436 6

**A Freshman Survival Guide for College Students
with Autism Spectrum Disorders**
The Stuff Nobody Tells You About!
Haley Moss
ISBN 978 1 84905 984 8
eISBN 978 0 85700 922 7

**Helping Students with Autism Spectrum Disorder
Express their Thoughts and Knowledge in Writing**
Tips and Exercises for Developing Writing Skills
Elise Geither and Lisa Meeks
ISBN 978 1 84905 996 1
eISBN 978 0 85700 980 7

COLLEGE

FOR STUDENTS
WITH DISABILITIES

WE DO BELONG

EDITED BY PAVAN JOHN ANTONY AND STEPHEN M. SHORE
FOREWORD BY TEMPLE GRANDIN

Jessica Kingsley *Publishers*
London and Philadelphia

First published in 2015
by Jessica Kingsley Publishers
73 Collier Street
London N1 9BE, UK
and
400 Market Street, Suite 400
Philadelphia, PA 19106, USA

www.jkp.com

Library of Congress Cataloging in Publication Data
College for students with disabilities : we do belong / edited
by Pavan John Antony and Stephen M. Shore.
     pages cm
  Includes bibliographical references and index.
  ISBN 978-1-84905-732-5 (alk. paper)
  1. College students with disabilities. 2. People with disabilities-
-Education (Higher) 3. Learning disabled--Education
(Higher) I. Antony, Pavan John. II. Shore, Stephen M.
  LC4818.38.C65 2015
  378.0087--dc23

                         2015012386

British Library Cataloguing in Publication Data
A CIP catalogue record for this book is available from the British Library

ISBN 978 1 84905 732 5
eISBN 978 1 78450 101 3

Printed and bound in the United States

Contents

This chapter highlights the experiences of eight individuals with cerebral palsy (CP) who graduated from different colleges. The individuals share their successes and challenges faced during their time in college. The transition from high school and the various factors that motivated these individuals to pursue a college degree are also discussed. This chapter offers a lot of practical tips for parents or individuals with CP who plan to attend or pursue a college education after high school. The personal stories included provide rich information regarding the daily life experiences of individuals with CP who attended college.

Employing an autobiographical angle looking at the experiences of others on the autism spectrum, this chapter examines the development of recognition and support services for individuals with autism in higher education. Other areas looked at include how teaching strategies for those with autism in higher education can be embedded into the teaching curriculum as extensions of good teaching practice rather than special things that are done for just a small number of people.

This chapter highlights the author's experience as a person with a disability working in the helping profession that she hopes will stimulate readers, especially those who are helping professionals, to frankly discuss the role that they have played in discrimination against people with disabilities so that they may work toward change. The author has spastic quadriplegia, a subset of cerebral palsy. She is unable to walk without assistance and gets around using a motorized wheelchair, and with a limited range of motion in all her limbs. She earned her Bachelor's degree and a Master's degree in school psychology, and shares her daily life experiences in and outside of the college.

The chapter highlights a model program that has been helping students with autism spectrum disorder (ASD) in college. The Bridges to Adelphi Program (BAP), at Adelphi University in Garden City, New York, is designed as a multifaceted support program for Adelphi students who self-disclose with ASD, or other non-verbal learning disorders. The stories included in the chapter reveals the daily life experiences of students with autism in college campuses.

Voices from the Field: Experiences of Students Written in Their Own Words

A person with multiple disabilities in addition to autism, Melissa describes her abusive family life and difficulties in grade school. Like many with autism, Melissa's story of transitioning to college highlights her hard-won successes through accommodations and developing a greater understanding of herself.

Foreword

Individuals with various disabilities can succeed in college. When I went to Arizona State University in the early 1970s, I lived in a graduate student dorm that also housed students with disabilities. Arizona State was a leader in the early 1970s. One of my best friends at Arizona State was Gloria Tester, my roommate who was blind. She successfully completed a degree in music. Gloria always had a can-do attitude. She was a master at using a cane and she walked everywhere on campus.

Another good friend was Diane, who had severe rheumatoid arthritis, and she used an electric wheelchair. After she completed her degree, she became the disability specialist for ASU.

There were also two graduate students I was friends with who were probably undiagnosed Asperger's. I fit in with them because I was a social misfit. Since this was the early 1970s, providing facilities for students with disabilities was pioneering. None of the students who were officially in the disability program had a problem that affected either their mind or speech. Amputations were the most common disability.

The individuals who describe their experiences in this book have problems that in many ways are more severe than a physical disability. It made me sad to read their stories of being bullied and discriminated against. I was bullied in both high school and college. The only places I was not bullied were areas of shared interests. A social highlight of my time in college was being in the school talent show, where I sang a silly song and made scenery. I am a big proponent of getting involved with shared interests because they were my main social life. Another shared interest in college was a CB radio club. It was a nerd Aspie heaven.

Temple Grandin
Author of The Autistic Brain *and* Thinking in Pictures

Introduction

Pavan John Antony and Stephen M. Shore

Introduction

"You are not college material" or "You don't belong in college" are comments that are frequently made to students with disabilities by many people in our society. Today, individuals with these same disabilities are being encouraged to enroll in higher education institutions across the United States and other countries, and the concept for this book evolved as both authors started teaching and advising college students with diverse abilities at Adelphi University, New York.

The students shared their daily experiences, encouraging us to make sure that their stories are told to the outside world in their own voices. This book highlights the stories of individuals with different types of disabilities who attended higher education—a model program developed for people with autism and related conditions at Adelphi University in New York is a highlight.

The book is a collection of stories written by scholars and individuals with disabilities regarding their experiences and insights for promoting their success in higher education. The editors have incorporated several chapters written by individuals with disabilities, expressing their experiences in their own voices. We felt the need to incorporate this ideology based on the philosophy that all voices need to be heard.

Today, college education for individuals with disabilities is becoming an expected part of transitioning for many people. By paving the way for students with disabilities to enter higher education, we are creating a bridge for students to continue their formal education in inclusive settings after high school. These opportunities lay the foundations for many of these people to build on their self-esteem and confidence, and to prove to the outside world that they have the same capacities as everyone else to achieve success in higher education.

The Americans with Disabilities Act of 1990 focuses, in part, on preparing students with disabilities for college through interview preparation, help with applications or supporting documents, and accessing accommodations in higher education. However, teachers and professionals continue to use a deficit rather than an abilities-based model when developing transition plans for students with disabilities, forcing many with disabilities to move into segregated environments or other situations that are below their capacities.

An important aspect of this book functions as a tool for readers to hear from, reflect on, and make personal decisions based on the findings of the researchers in collaboration with stories from people with disabilities regarding their own experiences in higher education.

College Experience

Individuals with Cerebral Palsy

Pavan John Antony, Assistant Professor of Special
Education, Adelphi University, New York

This chapter highlights the college experiences of nine individuals with cerebral palsy (CP) who attended different universities on the East Coast of the United States. The findings included derived from a study that was conducted by the lead editor. The main purpose of the study was to understand the daily experiences of those individuals in a higher education institution. The findings reveal that all the participants gained a higher level of self-confidence and maturity through their experience in higher education. The findings also highlight the various challenges that the participants faced, before, during, and after college.

Introduction

Attending college continues to be one of the biggest dreams for many high school graduates. It is typical for students in high school to start preparing for this transition by visiting local colleges and learning about the various programs offered in their areas of interest. Whereas these procedures are common practice among typically developing individuals, in contrast, most students with disabilities prepare themselves for transition into work settings or vocational training environments. It is typical for students with disabilities to continue in substantially separate special education programs after the age of 18 instead of going to college or technical school or full-time employment (Hart, Zimbrich, and Parker 2005). In addition, workforces or training centers for people with disabilities graduating from high school are usually in segregated settings, resulting in their exclusion from higher education, employment with their typically developing peers, and from their communities. In other words, a large number of students with disabilities remain invisible from the general public after graduating from high school.

Over the past few years there have been increased efforts to improve the transition for individuals with disabilities from high school to employment or towards pursuing college or professional training. Today, students with disabilities are increasingly enrolling in college campuses to receive a degree in higher education (Eckes and Ochoa 2005; Thomas 2000). According to Thomas (2000), between 1991 and 1996, the number of freshmen who reported having a disability increased by 10 percent, with most of the recorded disabilities being health impairment, hearing problem, learning disability, sight impairment, and speech impairment. According to a US Department of Education report in 2011, 88 percent of colleges enrolled students with disabilities: 31 percent of the students had learning disabilities, 18 percent had attention deficit disorder (ADD) and attention deficit hyperactivity disorder (ADHD), 18 percent had physical health conditions, 15 percent had mental or psychiatric conditions, 7 percent had difficulty hearing or seeing, and 11 percent had some other type of disability.

Today there is an increase in the number of school age children identified with various disabilities, suggesting that the number of students with disabilities entering college will also rise in the upcoming days. There is lack of data that provides the exact number of students with CP who are enrolled in colleges across the country. CP is a classification under physical disability, a majority group in college campuses across the US.

Cerebral palsy

CP refers to a group of non-progressive disorders, resulting from lesions or anomalies of the brain early in development (Rosenbaum *et al.* 2006). According to Rosenbaum *et al.*, these disorders are often accompanied by "disturbances of sensation, perception, cognition, communication, and behavior, by epilepsy, and by secondary musculoskeletal problems" (p.9). Many individuals with CP use wheelchairs or crutches, owning to their mobility impairment. Research informs us that many of these individuals may develop musculoskeletal problems, sensory problems like seizures, hearing or vision impairments, or communicative, attention, behavioral and/or cognitive deficits (Rosenbaum *et al.* 2006). They might also need frequent medical or personal attention, depending on the type and severity of the CP. It is important, however, that all professionals recognize the intellectual talents in many children with CP, as only part of their brain is affected. Today, individuals with CP continue to face challenges in various settings: public places (Engel-Yeger *et al.* 2009; Stewart *et al.* 2012), leisure activities (Majnemer 2010; Majnemer *et al.* 2008), and social activities such as dating, engaging in romantic or sexual relationships or (Majnemer *et al.* 2010). Irrespective of the lack of frequent participation by students with CP in activities outside of schools, young people with CP express enjoyment similar to typically developing peers (Engel-Yeger *et al.* 2009). Technology has also played an important role in helping students with disabilities smoothly transition into college or other careers (Burgstahler 2003, 2005).

Post-secondary education

Post-secondary education or transition after high school for individuals with disabilities is an area that is well researched (Getzel and Wehman 2005; Michelsen *et al.* 2005; Rothstein 1997; Thomas 2000; Wehman 2006; Wehman and Yasuda 2005). Today, more individuals with disabilities are seeking admission into colleges than ever before. Research reveals that more males with disabilities who are freshmen attend four-year institutions compared to females (Wehman and Yasuda, 2005). The reasons for low enrollment of female students with disabilities is still unknown. Wehman and Yasuda (2005) have highlighted that a college education could help an individual with higher earnings, stable benefits, career advancement, higher status and marketability in the field. They consider this to be one of the factors encouraging all indivduals to attend college. Today there is a lack of research regarding the experiences of individuals with CP who attend colleges and their life after graduation.

Studies have been conducted to determine the benefits of post-secondary educational programs for individuals with disabilities (Hart *et al.* 2004). Hart *et al.* looked at three separate educational programs—substantially separate, mixed, and inclusive—found at university level at the University of Kansas and the University of Hawaii at Manoa. They concluded that within the substantially separate program, individuals were mainly taught daily life skills that allowed them the opportunity to become employed in jobs such as maintenance or food preparation. Within the mixed program, individuals were not secluded from interacting with typically developing students. The main focus of instruction also pertains to life skills, and individuals were employed in similar jobs to those of individuals in the substantially separate program. Finally, the inclusive program is based on the individual's preferences and interests (person-centered), and they are provided with employment opportunities based on these interests. These post-secondary programs that are available to individuals with disabilities have increased the percentage of disabled individuals who find employment (Hart *et al.* 2004).

Another transition program, used in Midwest Community College, provided positive outcomes for individuals with disabilities who attended the program (Ankeny and Lehmann 2010). There were four participants in the study, and all benefited greatly from the program. One individual with a learning disability used the transition program to learn skills for becoming a foreman. Through his dedication within the program, he was successfully employed in a shop as a foreman. Another participant in the program with a mild mental disability gained employment as a phone transcriber, explaining that if it wasn't for this program, "I don't think I would be where I am now. I mean, I would have high school education with few computer classes and most places don't want to hire you if haven't had at least some college education…and I don't think I would even try to leave home without college or…I'd probably still be living with my parents if I didn't go on" (quoted in Ankeny and Lehmann 2010, p.485). Another individual with a mild mental disability is now an employee at a community hospital and is living independently. Although high school was a struggle for him, the encouragement of his special education teachers and mother enabled him to attend community college. He learned work-related skills, as well as skills that would enable him to live an independent life through college. Most importantly, he explained that the college had helped him to make friends, and he started interacting with other people. A fourth participant who wanted to become a teacher explained that because of her diagnosis of mild mental disability, her mother and Individualized Education Program (IEP) team always discouraged her from attending college because they felt it was unrealistic for her. She fought against them, and insisted that they help her find a program that would enable her to become a teacher. Today, she is a lead teacher for a pre-school program at a church in her community. During her education at Midwest Community College, field trips were a growing experience for her, and allowed her to "expand her knowledge of the world" (quoted in Ankeny and Lehmann 2010). These programs are only a few examples of how post-secondary education has given positive opportunities for individuals with disabilities to enter the workforce, and to become independent individuals.

It is important to acknowledge that post-secondary education is the next step to strengthen inclusion for individuals with disabilities graduating from high school. It provides equal opportunities for all learners graduating from high school. The above stories and the case studies discussed later in this chapter support the need for creating educational opportunities for students with disabilities graduating from high school. These true stories should help readers understand the lives of individuals with CP, before, during, and after a college education.

Purpose of the study

The purpose of the research was to expand knowledge regarding the experiences of individuals with CP attending college. Because the current literature has focused mostly on individuals with a learning disability, ADHD, or other mild disabilities, the researcher wanted to learn about the particular experiences of individuals with CP.

Methodology

This study was designed as a qualitative descriptive phenomenology in which the participants and the researcher engaged in semi-structured in-depth interviews (Creswell 1998). A phenomenological approach helps in understanding the rich experiences of individuals with CP who attend college. Interviews were used to collect data, as stories of people can give access to social and education issues in our society (Seidman 2013). This convenience sample included nine individuals with CP. The researcher contacted three local organizations to recruit individuals with CP, who were initially contacted via email. The researcher explained the study to the participants during a face-to-face meeting. Written consent was obtained from all the participants who volunteered to participate prior to interview. All the interviews were conducted at a time and a place that was convenient for the participants. For confidentiality, all the names used in this chapter are pseudonyms.

Data analysis

The method of analysis was essentially inductive and reflexive in nature, where the theory emerges from the data rather than from a predetermined focus (Patton 1990). All themes emerged from the coding categories generated through multiple readings of the interview data. Transcribed interview data were color-coded, and margin notes were made. Related ideas and concepts were grouped and categories and subcategories were developed; these were then analyzed using in-depth, cross-case analysis (Patton 1990). Member checks were conducted, and the interview transcriptions and findings were shared with the participants to establish credibility and validity. Participants were given the opportunity to add or edit the information as needed.

Findings

The participants shared their invaluable experiences, and several themes emerged that were new and some that supported the existing literature. These themes highlighted the experiences of participants before, during, and after college.

Transition experiences from high school

All the participants shared that they had had good experiences in their schools. However, they had had mixed experiences regarding their transition from high school. Eight out of nine participants shared that they had not been informed about attending college as a possibility prior to transitioning from high school. Two shared that it was their personal interest that had motivated them to attend college. Jen was the first and Salena the second person in her family to earn a college degree. Salena decided to pursue college based on her own personal motivation. According to her, "I have a physical limitation...cannot use my arms and legs well...the only way to succeed is to use my brain... I also wanted to learn how to protect myself and my sister with a disability." Salena's parents had taught her from childhood that her power was in her brain and not in her arms or legs. Salena believes that her parents' advice and motivation were some of the biggest factors that had motivated her to pursue college. She was told by one of her teachers that she was "not college material and not to pursue college." However, she succeeded in earning a Bachelor's in communication and rhetoric studies. She is currently planning to pursue a Master's in social work. Jen shares, "I was able to do everything in life only because of my family...my mom, she is the one who helped me with everything... God bless her... I wouldn't be anywhere near college without her."

Both Namy and Erma had siblings who had attended college, which was one of the other motivating factors for them to pursue college themselves. Namy decided to attend college when her classmates from high school mentioned their plans to attend college. Namy shared, "my family did not support me initially... but they changed their mind later." According to Erma:

> Academics was always an area of strength for me...it was kind of never really a question whether I would go to college...teachers always made me feel comfortable...and when I got to college I continued to enjoy the academic experiences...but [the] social piece was missing, just like in high school.

According to Ken, school professionals had tried hard to help him transition into real life, to "live in an apartment or find a job but did not help with getting into college...it was my own random networking, parent support and visiting colleges that got me into college."

Mary shared that her parents only wanted her typically developing brother and sister to attend college. According to Mary, her parents did not believe in her managing a college education. However, she wanted "to be treated the same like her siblings and not different." She also had a strong feeling that going to college would open up more opportunities than not attending any post-secondary institution. Mary further shared the advice from her guidance counselor to pursue college. According to her, "the guidance counselor had a nephew who had cerebral palsy who went to college and she's the one who told me about special services that certain colleges had at that time." Mary strongly believes that the counselor would not have thought college an option for her if he did not have a family member with CP.

Mic, who has spastic CP, shared the advice he had received from his high school social workers. The social workers had told Mic, "you shouldn't attend college because you don't have the ability to do certain custodial things...cleaning your backside after a bowel movement...dressing without help, tying sneakers." Mic's response was "I kind of looked at the social workers as though they were crazy. And two weeks later had my own transition plan written for the social worker...and said here, this is where I am going to go. This is how I'm doing it."

Teachers in high school had told six of the participants who used a special communication board that, being unable to communicate verbally and using a communication board would be the biggest barrier in attending college. Hardy shared, "they think am not able to compete with normal people since I use a communication device." He further shared, "my high school teachers were great... I do not think they even thought about me going to college."

Ken did a lot of personal research with the support of his parents. He shared, "I know that am not cognitively impaired... I scored a 3.89 GPA in college...but I remember my guidance counselor telling me that college is not an ideal place for me to succeed." Ken decided to pursue college when he found out that his high school classmates were pursuing college degrees. He shared "I earned my college degree through hard work...no one in school could even dream of me attending or completing college education...I did it."

All the participants shared that they had selected their colleges only after visiting several campuses. Ken did not like three colleges he had visited mainly owing to accessibility issues. He was also looking for a college that was closer to home. He decided not to attend one of the colleges he visited, as he did not enjoy the "interview process... I did not feel welcome." During

Erma's visit to a campus, she noticed that in one of the buildings, the door that was next to the ramp was locked with a chain. She shared "I have no idea why it was chained… I waited, waited and waited…my group leader who was giving us a tour called the security and they unlocked it later… I did not pick that college… I had no idea why it was chained." Bob decided to attend college only four years after graduating from high school. No one at his high school had advised him to pursue a college education.

College experiences
INITIAL DAYS IN COLLEGE

The participants shared mixed feelings regarding their first day of class: nervous, thrilled, excited, and scared, to name a few. Six participants shared that they were nervous during the first day of class. Ken and his personal care attendant (PCA) could not find his class and he was late to the first day of class. Jen shared her first semester experience as, "a complete disaster… I was in the wrong building and it was my fault." She shared that her professor had told all the students on the first day "not to come into class if you are more than five minutes late." She was late to class during the second week because of her "Able Ride," the local company that arranges free rides for individuals with disabilities. She was not allowed in the class. According to Jen, "my professor is a nice person and the rule applied to all students…when I explained my situation, she asked me to come in early…but I said I couldn't as there was no bus before 6.30 am…the professor was tough and I argued with her for weeks."

Namy, on the other hand, arrived 15 minutes early to the first class and shared her experience as feeling excited as well as nervous. She also shared that she had made a few friends on the first day. According to Namy, she had initiated all the conversations with her classmates. She believed that getting to all her classes several minutes early was a tool she had adopted throughout her college education.

Mic explained his first day of class:

I remember me being very jittery but very excited just like everyone else…one of the first things I remember was being able to look around the campus as a 19-year-old kid and see girls…granted I saw them at my high school, but this environment was different… I felt special…it was awesome… I made it to college… I was proud of myself.

Mary couldn't remember her first day of class. However, she shared about a placement test that she had taken within the first few weeks of classes. "I was supposed to get extended time on the test, but for some reason I got messed up, so I didn't do very well on the placement test. So they placed me in the BEP, which is called the Basic Education Program…which is sort of for people who are up to college level but are not quite there yet… So I was misplaced in that program." Mary decided to stay in the program as she was unaware of the steps involving entering the correct program. According to Namy, every day in college was a new learning experience, filled with surprises and challenges.

Hardy was scared after his first calculus class. According to him, "the professor assigned [a] bunch of work on the first day with no accommodations… I was slow to respond and he didn't seem to care." By the end of the first class, the calculus professor asked Hardy's PCA, "Will Hardy be able to get through the semester…?" Hardy's PCA responded by stating "He is here to learn." Hardy had to find his own note-taker on the first day, and his PCA helped him find a note-taker for all his classes.

Bob met with some of his professors after his first class. He identified his note-takers by himself. He shared that not all students were willing to be note-takers, and that he had to keep asking several students until he found someone to help. Bob shared:

On the first few days everyone in my class thought [I] am retarded or someone who is not capable, but when I started answering questions, I saw students looking at me with surprise… I felt proud and intellectually competent, like one of them…a normal person.

Salena completed all her paperwork prior to the first day of her class, and explained to all her professors the accommodations she needed. She also shared an incident where one of the professors had questioned her about an accommodation. According to Salena, the professor asked her during the third week "Why do you need this accommodation? You do not look disabled enough...the questions are straightforward and simple." Salena made an appointment with the professor to explain about her disability and why she needed the accommodations.

Erma shared that her first day in college had gone smoothly. She stated that her transition to college had only gone smoothly because she had completed advance placement classes during her high school education. According to her:

> When I was in high school I took a lot of AP [Advanced Placement] classes...so I managed to move a lot of hard stuff out of the way...these are college-level classes in high school, and if you get a certain grade on the AP tests...you can get college credits for it so you won't have to take it when you get to college...no one told me to take this route, but I wanted to...

Erma later shared that the head of the psychology department had taught her first class, and she considered him one of the best professors on the campus. She also stated that she took several classes from the same professor during her course of study. According to Erma, "it's rare for me to like all people...but this professor knew what he was teaching...he was my advisor."

COLLEGE AND THE LEARNING PROCESS

All the participants in the study shared that college education had helped them to be stronger. Mic shared that he felt more mature after earning a college degree.

All of them shared that they had gained mastery in their field of study during their college education. Ken believed that he had learned many socially acceptable practices through his college education. According to Bob, the college classroom was the only place where he was challenged intellectually. This belief was supported by all the other participants in the study. Hardy, who struggled with several medical issues, completed his degree, albeit taking 16 years. He shared, "I finally did it… I proved that [I] am college material… I feel good." Hardy was not at all worried about the number of years it had taken for him to complete his education. He continued to advocate and encourage students with CP graduating from high school to consider college education as an option. He shared, "it's a unique experience that you will never forget."

According to seven participants, managing time was a skill that they learned within the first few weeks of classes. Mic considered managing time as one of the key ingredients to succeeding in college. According to Salena, "it takes anywhere from an hour 30 minutes or more for me to get ready in the morning…but I have to be on time for class." Salena shared that she was always on time for classes and appointments. Seven participants in this study shared that it took more than two hours for them to complete the basic activities of living and to get ready for school in the morning. According to Bob, "if my class starts at 9.00 am… I wake up before 5.00 am ." Six participants who were dependent on PCAs for their care talked about the role of PCAs in helping them be on time for classes on a regular basis. Mic had had bad experiences with three PCAs as some of them had come in late and some had not made any personal connection. According to Mic, "I finally decided to conduct an interview for selecting my PCA, and that's when I got Sammy, who has been with me for the past six years…he is great." Mic stated that if it was not for being on time for his classes, he would not have thought about conducting an interview to select his PCA.

Understanding rights

All the participants highlighted that they had learned about their legal rights only after starting classes at their respective colleges. Three participants, Mic, Mary, and Namy, shared that they had learned about several of the accommodations and their legal rights mainly from their friends with disabilities in college. Salena believed that not being aware of any of her legal rights had been a big mistake on her part. She shared an example that no one had informed her about getting a grade of "Incomplete" for a course during a semester. She was enrolled in a program that helped college students with disabilities in the campus, and was upset about the fact that irrespective of paying a special fee to be in the program, she had not been educated or informed about several of her rights. Salena also shared that her parents had purchased books on tapes for her to attend classes, and that she had not been informed about this accommodation by anyone in school. She was unaware of her rights, and learned of them only after networking with other college students with disabilities. She also believed that while professionals, teachers, and parents take an active role in protecting the rights of children at school, they failed to educate them regarding the legal system or rights for people with disabilities graduating from high school.

Ken admitted that he advocated for his own rights for the first time after being in college. According to Ken, "I do not think I would have been able to advocate for myself without my experiences in college... I strongly felt the need to seek my rights." Hardy shared that disability support office staff in campus are the ultimate decision-makers for students with disabilities in any campuses. Bob shared that he read books and conducted research to learn about his rights.

Jen was unaware of any of her legal rights prior to attending college. She shared that, "parents and teachers [do] everything for you and I never thought about laws or rights in school." She was forced to learn about her legal rights in college when her fieldwork placement was delayed for more than two months at three different places owing to lack of accessibility. According to her, "there were no accessible toilets at my first field placement building... I couldn't turn my wheelchair around the stall...no elevator at the second place...no accessible doors." Jen could not finish some of her coursework on time on account of this issue, and had to self-advocate for her placement in an accessible building/community. Jen shared that "most people who worked in the disability office were able-bodied and they place people like us without thinking about accessibility." She shared that learning about her legal rights and fighting for them had made her a stronger person. She also shared that these types of issues were ongoing, and blamed university officials for what she saw as their irresponsibility.

Erma learned about rights and legal systems in special education only after starting graduate school. She was aware of her IEP in school, but lacked knowledge regarding any other rights. She also shared that she attended only one Committee on Special Education (CSE) meeting in ninth grade during her entire life.

Namy was part of a self-advocacy group on campus where she learned about her legal and student rights. She shared that, "one of my teachers at the college knew that it took me a while to read the assignment, so she called me and suggested that I could qualify for getting the books on tapes." Namy mentioned that she would not have been aware of this accommodation without this professor's advice. All the participants admitted that they had gained knowledge about their rights mainly though their own personal research and through social networks.

Friends and college

Namy and Mic were the only two participants who made friends during the first week of classes. They believed that this had happened because they had initiated most of the conversations. According to Mic, "I let people around me know that [I] am a social person and am capable of doing things like they are... I believe this is important for me to make friends and thrive in a college setting."

Six participants who used a communication board shared that there was little to no communication with their classmates during the first few weeks of classes. However, two participants engaged in brief conversations, asking questions and responding to "yes" or "no" answers. Two had not engaged in any detailed conversations with fellow classmates during the entire semester.

Seven participants shared that they had not made friends without disabilities during their entire time in college. Seven had never been invited to social events by their fellow classmates during their time in college. All the participants mentioned that they spent most of their time with individuals with disabilities during their free hours in college and during weekends. Mic, on the other hand:

> Socialized with classmates by asking them to help me get a book out or asking them to slide a table or pull chairs out so that I could come in with my wheelchair. Most of them would instinctually do it and then say nothing. But then you'd initiate the conversation with a thank you and the conversation would continue. I didn't socialize much my first semester or first year. My only socialization was literally at my cousin's football games at XX University and that would be with my family...but I have invited people to my room if I can't make it to a pub... We would get it done another way. But I should say it was difficult...

Mic was also made fun of by his friends without disabilities while dating an "able-bodied person." Mic had friends who made comments like "he doesn't want to date one of his own." Mic responded, saying, "We are all humans." According to Mic, these comments had created "insecurity in his relationship." Mic believes that these experiences, along with regular classes and college work, had made him a stronger person. He considered that his decision to attend college had been one of the best decisions he had ever made in his life. This was an argument that was supported by all the participants in the study.

Hardy's classmates never invited him to any social events. He believed that it was hard for him to be anywhere without his PCA, "I am dependent on him for using restrooms, moving around campus and for everything." Hardy believed that lack of independence was one of the factors limiting people with disabilities from developing friendships in college. Bob considered lack of transportation as one of the biggest factors restricting people like him from socializing. According to Bob, "there is no transportation for attending late night events...what can we do... I can never travel in a car as my wheelchair won't fit in... there is no way people like me can be out after a certain time."

According to Jen:

> I grew up with friends who are able-bodied and most of my niece's friends that know me are able-bodied, but I tend to gravitate toward disabled because...you don't have to explain anything, like when I am having a bad spasm day...it's easy to joke around with my friends who have disabilities by saying it's a bad spas day or, you know, just joke around about it and then we could move on to the next subject...on the other hand, I remember students without disabilities asking me, oh my god, are you ok, and I'm like, I'm fine! This is my daily life, this is what I sometimes go through, whether I like it or not...

Namy stated that she had made friends in college, but "they were all classroom friends." She shared, "there were several incidences where I tried to communicate with students and they either shy away or talk down, at least [a] few of them...they don't realize how much I am capable of or what can I offer." Namy had one friend in college who had a sibling with a disability. According to her, "she was good and this girl visited me at my home twice... she connected with me because she has a sibling who also has a disability." Namy felt that college students without disabilities did not have any basic understanding of CP or any disability among their fellow classmates. This lack of understanding led to the development of a wall of segregation between "able-bodied and people like us in colleges." Namy believed that students with CP would continue to face these kinds of challenges in the absence of a proper disability education system in colleges.

Salena shared that she initiated most of the conversations with her classmates, as "I needed help...most of my fellow students aren't really talking to me...I don't know why." Salena shared that she had made friends but had lost them as she did not stay in touch, especially when she was not feeling well due to medical issues and other personal reasons. She had no PCA and was dependent on her mother for help. She struggled with finding friends or college students who could help her with basic things like grocery shopping, folding laundry, and getting out and about. Although she had offered to pay someone, she had not found anyone, and continued to seek her mother's help. She shared, "there were days when I couldn't balance physical therapy with my classes...my mornings were bad and [I] couldn't move around... I did not have [a] good coping mechanism to deal with these types of situations... I have locked myself in my room for days and once almost for two weeks...it was my mom who helped me at that time...the school was small, but no one contacted me." Salena also shared that she was unable to participate in a study abroad program to Greece as there were no accommodations for individuals with disabilities. According to her, "I posted fliers, contacted several friends... I offered to pay for anyone to go to Greece, pay X amount as salary...all you need to do for three weeks is sit in the classroom and take my notes...no one volunteered...there was no help or initiative from the study abroad office either."

Mary shared that she had asked students around her for help as needed. She believed that it had helped her with graduating from college. According to her, "I enjoyed college life from the day one... I learned the reality that college classmates are not [the] same as your schoolmates...they came into classes and were rushing for the next...no time to interact or chat... I decided to ask them for extra help...asking my friend to help me with my homework when needed...especially with the math part... I had a classmate who was also a teacher...she explained to me and helped me...and I did good... I had [a] few students who ignored me after I asked them [to] help...one student changed seat...but it was the one student who was the teacher who was ready to help me anytime... I was lucky."

According to Erma:

I should say that the people in college were a little bit nicer in class but, like I said, I did try to do things with students outside of class...socially...it didn't follow through when I wasn't on campus and...that was a very frustrating thing for me because I didn't understand what was going on because I had people's numbers and things like that...we would potentially make plans to go to a movie or something and when I would call or text to like actually set it up...they would just, like, ignore it...and I was, like... I don't get why...because you know I am not a mean person... I know that [I] am a person with limitations like needing help if we go out and I need to use a restroom...do basic things...

Barriers inside and outside the classroom

All the participants enjoyed their college experiences and shared various challenges they had faced during their college education, which ranged from working with PCAs to completing assignments on time. Six participants mentioned that they had not met their academic advisors before the first day of classes. Three never met their advisor in person. According to Bob "it was not a requirement...nobody told me to take an appointment with the advisor." Jen decided to enroll for some harder classes at the beginning, and shared that it had not been her best decision. Salena enrolled for classes with the help of one of her friends, and used her program of study sheet as a reference. All the participants who had not met their academic advisor at the beginning of their school semester shared this as a mistake on their part. The participants also highlighted that they had received too much information via email and paper prior to beginning college.

Seven participants had been assisted by their PCA or parents to get to their classes. The PCAs helped with performing most of the activities of daily living, such as using the toilet, taking a shower, dressing, and getting ready for the day. All the participants shared several incidences where college students or professors asked the PCAs questions instead of asking the participants. Jen, who did not have a PCA, shared that it took three hours for her to get ready for college in the morning. She considered this as her routine. According to Jen, "my mom serves as my PCA, counselor, mentor, and sometimes my driver." Nancy and Mary took less than two hours to get ready for college.

The participants shared mixed feeling regarding their PCAs. Mic pointed out that when a person has difficulty communicating, most people avoid talking, or find another easier way, and that was asking the PCA. Other participants in the study supported this. According to Mic, "I am at a point where I would ask my PCA to leave me outside of an employer's main office instead of pushing me into his office for an interview... I let them push me and usually try to talk to them and make a personal connection." All the participants who used communication devices shared that their professors had not been aware of their specific disability.

Life after graduation

Hardy, Bob, Namy, and Ken currently work at a program for individuals with CP, and serve as teaching assistants. They are also actively involved with advocating for the rights of individuals with disabilities in their program and in the community. Salena plans to go on to higher education. Mary has attended several job interviews after graduating from college. She shared about her special interest in helping people during her interviews, but rarely heard back from many. She was once denied a job as a greeter because she could not stand for long hours. According to Mary, "I use crutches, but in order to avoid spasms that could happen by standing for longer hours, I wanted to use a wheelchair...they didn't like that...so they said I couldn't have the job because I needed to sit down to greet them...they wanted me standing... that's what I say, close-mindedness."

According to Mic:

> I sent out 2127 résumés in the past four years…gotten
> approximately 50 interviews…but the biggest challenge
> in any aspect of life is to just continue to be who I am. A lot
> of people with disabilities will shy away. They get angry.
> They withdraw. They isolate. I've gone through that a lot
> as well… I still continue to look for opportunities…

Mic volunteers at local organizations, and has been tutoring
college students. He has also been guest lecturing at local
educational institutions and organizations.

Jen was offered positions at two different schools, but could
not accept the job offer owing to lack of accessibility. She shared,
"I was told if a kid breaks his limb by accident, he/she has to go
to a nearby school that is accessible."

Erma, who earned her counseling degree, works part time
at a local university. She was also interviewed at a local school
district for a counselor position, but was unsuccessful due to the
lack of accessibility. The interview was conducted in 2014, at a
school that had no elevator.

Discussion

The stories discussed in this chapter clearly support the fact
that those with CP transitioning from high school are not fully
informed about the possibility of pursuing higher education in
colleges or universities after graduating from college. Lack of
expectation from teachers, administrators, and career counselors
at high school is already an issue that has been raised (Wehman
and Yasuda 2005). There are several intervention approaches
transition teams can use to assist students with disabilities in
successfully entering college. Flexer *et al.* (2008) include an
approach known as "backward planning" which allows the team
to start planning the transition from the time the individual
graduates to the present time, where the individual is. One
of these approaches involves the individual with disabilities

becoming completely independent as an adult (Kochhar-Bryant and Greene 2008). During this approach their high school education will be based entirely on entering higher education, becoming independent as an adult and in the community, and participating in work-related activities as well as employment opportunities in high school. Another approach that Kochhar-Bryant and Greene (2008) suggest is having the individual with disabilities receive a high school education involving academic and career courses, assisting them in attending a vocational school, or participating in a career apprenticeship after graduating. Both these approaches help individuals become independent members of the community, successfully obtaining employment.

These stories are powerful testimonies by individuals who have successfully completed college, irrespective of their disability. It is important for all of us to acknowledge that post-secondary education enables individuals with CP to build self-confidence, gives them opportunities to strengthen and build their self-determination skills, and provides them with job opportunities, self-awareness skills, and self-advocacy skills. The formation of these skills has allowed individuals with disabilities to have a brighter future. Post-secondary education programs provide experiences simulating real-life situations so that individuals can practice the responsibilities of employment and of adult roles (Ankeny and Lehmann 2010).

There is no doubt that post-secondary education offers many benefits for individuals with CP, but it is equally important to acknowledge the reality that many of these individuals face challenges in securing a job on graduation, the main reasons being lack of accessibility at workplaces, lack of awareness among employers regarding individuals with CP, and the continued negative attitude toward individuals with disabilities among the public. The challenge of securing a job by individuals with CP on graduation is not only a challenge in the USA, but is also an international issue. For example, studies conducted by a group of scholars from Denmark highlight the lack of jobs for individuals with CP (Michelsen *et al.* 2005). This is also evident in countries such as India (Antony 2010).

This is the time for all of us to come forward and plant the seed of inclusion outside of the school community. All students graduating from high school should be well informed regarding their legal rights and opportunities to attend college after graduation. Employers and community members need to be educated regarding the talents and strengths among college graduates with CP. We should not assume that all individuals with CP who cannot talk, walk, or who use a wheelchair are not capable of performing things like typically developing people in our society. If individuals like Hardy can gain a college degree after 16 years, there is no doubt that these individuals can complete any work assigned by their future employers.

References

Ankeny, E. and Lehmann, J.P. (2010) "The transition lynchpin: The voices of individuals with disabilities who attended a community college transition program." *Community College Journal of Research and Practice 34*, 6, 477–496.

Antony, P.J. (2010) *Segregation Hurts: Voices of Youth with Disabilities and their Families in India.* Rotterdam, Netherlands: Sense Publishers.

Burgstahler, S. (2003) "The role of technology in preparing youth with disabilities for postsecondary education and employment." *Journal of Special Education Technology 18*, 4, 7–19.

Burgstahler, S. (2005) "The role of technology in preparing for college and careers." In E.E. Getzel and P. Wehman (eds) *Going to College: Expanding Opportunities for People with Disabilities.* Baltimore, MD: Paul Brookes Publishing.

Creswell, J.W. (1998) *Qualitative Inquiry and Research Design. Choosing among Five Traditions.* Thousand Oaks, CA: Sage Publications.

Eckes, S.E. and Ochoa, T.A. (2005) "Students with disabilities: Transitioning from high school to higher education." *American Secondary Education 33*, 3, 6–20.

Engel-Yeger, B., Jarus, T., Anaby, D., and Law, M. (2009) "Differences in patterns of participation between youths with cerebral palsy and typically developing peers." *The American Journal of Occupational Therapy 63*, 1, 96–104.

Flexer, R.W., Baer, R.M., Luft, P. and Simmons, T.J. (2008). *Transition Planning for Secondary Students with Disabilities.* Upper Saddle River, NJ: Pearson.

Getzel, E.E and Wehman, P. (2005) *Going to College: Expanding Opportunities for People with Disabilities.* Baltimore, MD: Brookes Publishing Company.

Hart, D., Zimbrich, K., and Parker, D.R. (2005) "Dual enrollment as a postsecondary education option for students with intellectual disabilities." In E.E. Getzel and P. Wehman (eds) *Going to College: Expanding Opportunities for People with Disabilities*, pp. 253–267. Baltimore, MD: Paul Brookes Publishing Company.

Hart, D., Mele-McCarthy, J., Pasternack, R.H., Zimbrich, K., and Parker, D.R. (2004) "Community college: A pathway to success for youth with learning, cognitive, and intellectual disabilities in secondary settings." *Education and Training in Developmental Disabilities 39*, 1, 54–66.

Kochhar-Bryant, C.A. and Greene, G. (2008) *Pathways to Successful Transition for Youth with Disabilities: A Developmental Process*, 2nd edition. Upper Saddle River, NJ: Pearson.

Majnemer, A. (2010) "Balancing the boat: Enabling an ocean of possibilities." *Canadian Journal of Occupational Therapy 77*, 4, 198–208.

Majnemer, A., Shevell, M., Law, M., Birnbaum, R., *et al.* (2008) "Participation and enjoyment of leisure activities in school-aged children with cerebral palsy." *Developmental Medicine and Child Neurology 50*, 10, 751–758.

Majnemer, A., Shikako-Thomas, K., Chokron, N., Law, M., *et al.* (2010) "Leisure activity preferences for 6- to 12-year-old children with cerebral palsy." *Developmental Medicine and Child Neurology 52*, 2, 167–173.

Michelsen, S.I., Uldall, P., Anne Mette, T.K., and Madsen, M. (2005) "Education and employment prospects in cerebral palsy." *Developmental Medicine and Child Neurology 47*, 8, 511–517.

Patton, M.Q. (1990) *Qualitative Evaluation and Research Methods*, 2nd edn. Newbury Park, CA: Sage Publications.

Rosenbaum, P., Paneth, N., Leviton, A., Goldstein, M., *et al.* (2007) 'The Definition and Classification of Cerebral Palsy'. *Developmental Medicine & Child Neurology*, 49: 1–44. doi: 10.1111/j.1469-8749.2007.00001.x

Rothstein, L. (1997) "Higher education and disabilities: Trends and developments." *Stetson Law Review 27*, 119–138.

Seidman, I. (2013) *Interviewing as Qualitative Research: A Guide for Researchers in Education and the Social Sciences.* New York: Teachers College Press.

Stewart, D.A., Lawless, J.J., Shimmell, L.J., Palisano, R.J., *et al.* (2012) "Social participation of adolescents with cerebral palsy: Trade-offs and choices." *Physical & Occupational Therapy in Pediatrics 32*, 2, 167–179.

Thomas, S.B. (2000) "College students and disability law." *Journal of Special Education 30*, 4, 248–257.

US (United States) Department of Education (2011) *Students with Disabilities at Degree-granting Postsecondary Institutions: First Look.* Available at http://nces.ed.gov/pubs2011/2011018.pdf

Wehman, P. (2006) *Life Beyond the Classroom: Transition Strategies for Young People with Disabilities.* Baltimore, MD: Brookes Publishing Company.

Wehman, P. and Yasuda, S. (2005) "The Need and Challenges Associated with Going to College." In E.E. Getzel and P. Wehman (eds) *Going to College: Expanding Opportunities for People with Disabilities*, pp. 3–23. Baltimore, MD: Paul Brookes Publishing Company.

3

The Journey to Professorship on the Autism Spectrum

Stephen M. Shore, Clinical Assistant
Professor, Adelphi University, New York

As described by many in this book, I got through most of my studies in higher education without coming into contact with student support services or other assistance related to being on the autism spectrum. So little was known about autism at that time that it was assumed that anyone with autism would not be in college anyways, but rather in a supervised situation, and likely to be non-verbal. That said, I credit my parents who were forward thinking in terms of implementing what we today would refer to as a college transition program, a voracious curiosity as to how things worked, some splinter skills, and teachers who seemed to intuitively understand my learning differences—all glued together with a certain amount of just being in the right place at the right time.

School days

After 18 months of typical development, I was struck with what I refer to as the "autism bomb," where I lost functional communication, had meltdowns, and in short, became a severely affected child on the autism spectrum. Fortunately, my parents refuted professional recommendations from doctors claiming to never having seen a two-and-a-half-year-old child "so sick," and convinced the diagnostic team to enroll me in about a year. During that year my parents implemented what today would be referred to as an intensive home-based early intervention program, emphasizing movement, music, sensory integration, narration, and imitation. At a time when the concept of early intervention did not even exist, my parents just did what they felt needed to be done to connect with their child.

For example, when my parents' attempts to get me to imitate them failed, they flipped the technique around and began imitating me—upon which I became aware of them in my environment. Then they were able to move me along to where at age four speech began to return, and I began attending the center that originally recommended institutionalization. Upon re-evaluation I got upgraded from psychotic, atypical development and strong autistic tendencies to neurotic. Things were looking up.

Grade school

By age six my speech had pretty much normalized and I entered public school kindergarten where I was a social and academic catastrophe. For example, walking about the classroom repeating the letter "B" did not endear me to my classmates. I was usually about a grade behind in most of my subjects. Realizing this, I was often gratefully surprised when promoted to the next grade level instead of being kept back.

Rather than doing typical schoolwork, such as reading in groups or math, I spent most of my time in elementary school reading books on my favorite subjects such as aviation, space exploration, earthquakes, world history, electricity, and other subjects. All of these books, combined with the regular academic schedule, made school an interesting place to learn—and helped me tolerate the bullying, both by my classmates, and occasionally by my teachers as well. For example, one day in third grade I was deep in a study of astronomy, with multiple books strewn on my desk. I was taking notes and copying diagrams from those texts, and a teacher walked up, telling me that I'd never learn how to do math.

Somehow I have learned enough mathematics to teach statistics at university level. The good news is that today, an educator would have likely noticed my fascination with astronomy, and found a good way to teach math through this subject. Relatedly, I am seeing more educators developing sensitivity in teaching toward interests and learning styles. In general, people tend to learn better and faster about things they are interested in. It is in those interests that we often find a person's strengths. By combining awareness of interests and strengths with knowledge of students' learning styles, we can greatly improve student comprehension and mastery of subject material. Educators at all levels—pre-school through post-doctoral—will be more effective if they can address as many learning styles as possible when teaching subject matter. For example, the worksheet below, in Table 3.1, may be helpful in developing a lesson plan on the Pythagorean theorem as part of a mathematics unit.

Table 3.1: Applying Howard Gardner's eight intelligences for using the Pythagorean theorem to determine the length of the hypotenuse of a right triangle, when side A and B are known

8 Intelligences Planning Worksheet	
Subject:	Pythagorean theorem
Unit:	Measuring polygons
Plan:	Students develop material describing how to solve for the hypotenuse of a right triangle using the Pythagorean theorem
Assessment:	Mastery of and explanation of using the formula
Assignment	Please choose one of the following ways to describe how to use the Pythagorean theorem in determining the length of the hypotenuse of a right triangle for presentation to your classmates

Intelligence-learning focus	Related images	Directions
Verbal-linguistic (words)		Write a story or script out a monologue
Mathematical-logical (numbers)		Relate to numbers or calculations involved in arriving at your answer
Musical		Discuss a relevant song you heard or compose and perform a song
Visual-spatial (pictures)		Draw or paint in the style of a graphic novel, make a collage or poster
Bodily-kinesthetic (movement)		Show using movement
Interpersonal (communication)		Write a play or pretend news story to be delivered by you and one other classmate
Intrapersonal (self)		Present a journal or diary describing any changes of behavior, habits, or greater self-understanding in learning how to use the Pythagorean theorem

Naturalist (nature)		Describe what you learned about nature and caring for plants and/or animals

Middle and high school can be very challenging for many students, whether they have disabilities or not. In contrast, these upper grades were easier for me for three important reasons. First, I realized that using words instead of sound effects from the environment really helped with social interactions. Previously I would imitate sounds heard at home and elsewhere, with the hope of getting my classmates to imitate them back to me. Doing so was an easier and more predictable way of communication for me. Second, I slowly began to understand what teachers wanted from me in terms of completing assignments. All through grade school—especially in the lower grades—meeting teacher expectations was more about guessing what the teacher wanted in terms of class or homework, and hoping I was right. While meeting teacher expectations was easier for me in middle and high school, it was only on entering college that I felt I had a firm grasp on teacher (now professor) expectations. Whether it was due to differences in teaching style, development on my own, or some combination of both, I found myself thunderstruck when professors would tell the class exactly what they wanted their students to do for homework and for class projects.

Transition to college

No formal transition to college programs for individuals with autism and other disabilities existed when I started my undergraduate education. However, the experiences described below contain many elements found in today's efforts to effect smooth transitions from high school to college.

Ever since I knew that higher education existed, I was always fascinated by the idea of going to college. This desire grew after getting involved in the band in middle school, with music becoming an insatiable special interest, leading to me spending hours in the instrument closet figuring out how to play as many instruments as possible, and peppering my poor music teacher with endless questions about music theory and composition. My interest in music continued its expansion in high school.

"Take a few days off from school and go with your sister to college," my parents would occasionally tell me while I was in high school. College was a wonderland of learning, nice people, and no bullies. Even though I was my sister's "kid brother," the classes I visited with her were fun, and people seemed interested in what I was doing there, and even welcomed my input into the discussion. It was also cool to have classes outside—something that was never done in grade school. Upon returning to grade school after these excursions, with the realities of bullying and teachers having difficulty understanding me, I redoubled my efforts to make sure I would go to college after graduation.

Applications to college followed soon thereafter, my having chosen half a dozen possibilities. With three acceptances, I chose the same school that I had visited with my sister, and lived in the same dorm she was in, and selected a friend from high school with whom I attended incoming student orientation late in the Spring, before starting the following Fall, to be my roommate. I was doubly pleased to learn that the date of the orientation was during the senior prom, and was happy to have a valid excuse not to participate in this socially charged event.

With anticipation and my high school friend in the passenger seat, we eagerly pointed the car due west for a 90-mile trip to our new educational experience. With my friend majoring in communication and me in music, we spent little time together during those three days. Most of my time was spent getting to know the professors and the building where the music department was located, registering for courses, and meeting other incoming music students. One of those courses, Marching Band, included "Band Camp" for a full week before the beginning of school. The orientation was fairly uneventful, with both my friend and I looking forward to the beginning of the Fall semester as freshmen.

Yet another unintended component of my transition to college was attending "Band Camp" a week before the beginning of the semester. A full week living in the dorm, several hours of daily band practice, the dining commons, and interacting with new classmates helped increase my familiarity with the campus and develop long-lasting friendships. With another week on campus under my belt, I went home for Labor Day weekend to prepare for my upcoming first semester.

Internal and external models of support for transitioning to college

There are currently many programs for people on the autism spectrum and with other conditions helping to smooth the transition from high school to college. Some are based within the college itself, and can be considered *internal* to an institution of higher education, whereas others are *external* to university campuses.

Internal models are housed within higher education institutions, with services being provided on campus, except for off-campus excursions organized by the program. Examples of internal programs include the Bridges to Adelphi Program at Adelphi University in New York, and the College Program for Students with Asperger's Syndrome at Marshall University in West Virginia.

Another example of an internal model is the work being done with the Henry Viscardi School, located near the Adelphi University campus. This school provides support for children with severe physical disabilities in an accessible, traditional educational setting. In collaboration with Adelphi University, students from the school begin with short excursions to practice navigating the university campus. They then come to campus to attend class sessions taught by Viscardi teachers, before visiting classes taught by professors from Adelphi University. Introducing only one new aspect at a time helps with many types of transitioning to college.

In contrast, external programs are not associated with higher education institutions and have minimal contact with administration, faculty, and staff. They provide varying degrees of support and education in interdependent living for individuals on the autism spectrum who are already enrolled in, or planning to enroll in, higher education. Examples include the College Internship Program (CIP) and the College Living Experience (CLE); both have a number of branches around the United States.

The external model often involves individuals with autism sharing a house or apartment off-campus, with one or more roommates who also are on the autism spectrum. These programs provide support by educating these individuals on strategies to successfully navigate the challenges of living "on one's own" in conjunction with attending a college or university. Some areas of focus include schedule and financial management, maintaining proper nutrition, addressing use of leisure time, and involvement in the community. Another important area of focus is promoting a deeper understanding of what having autism means in terms of the student's success in education, and life in general.

Because these programs are external to colleges and universities, there is a substantial fee beyond what is paid for college tuition. This fee can reach upwards of $60,000 a year, whereas costs for the internal model are significantly less.

Similar programs also commonly exist for students with other disabilities.

Reaching utopia—college at last!

With the car packed with supplies and possessions, my friend and I headed to college and we moved into the dorm made familiar from my visits to my sister over the prior few years. On getting to the dorm it seemed like everyone was moving in at the same time. There were special places near the entrances where one could park their car if placards indicating "30 minutes" were displayed on the dashboard. Long waits for the elevator meant moving all my possessions from the car to the room was going to take much longer than the allotted time—but I also realized that everyone else was in the same position, and there was little chance of the car being towed away if it remained longer. Thinking back, I am sure the university staff were too busy to time how long vehicles were parked near the door as students emptied their cars and hauled their possessions to their dorm rooms.

College was something I had been looking forward to ever since I began my visits to my sister. The sharp contrast between very few of my classmates being willing to talk with me in grade school and the friendliness of my new dorm and fellow students was shocking. Never had I seen others my own age talk with each other, even if they were strangers.

Another poignant difference between grade school and college was that my classmates seemed to appreciate me for who I was, instead of making fun of me and bullying me for my differences. In short, I could just be myself. Whereas my special interest in bicycles was either ignored or made fun of in high school, I found many others at university who were also involved in bicycles. The possibility of engaging in my interest *with* my classmates rather than having to seek others outside the school community was very exciting to me. Playing and listening to classical music with others, or even going on midnight bicycle rides, was a dream come true.

Sharing the dorm room with my friend from high school was a helpful part of transitioning into college. At first we did most things together, except for going to our classes. After breakfast in the dining commons we'd go our separate ways and meet in the dorm room for lunch. Then we'd meet in the dining commons for dinner, with the evenings spent on homework and talking with others on the dorm floor. Gradually, our interests began to take us separate ways, and we'd spend less time together. My roommate was more interested in the typical nightlife of visiting fraternities and parties, whereas I preferred to either stay in the dorm room, practice trombone in the fine arts center, or spend the weekends away at home or at a friend's house.

After settling into my routines at college I began to think about employment. Mostly focused on being a security guard in one of the buildings or working in the dining commons, none of the campus-based work-study jobs appealed to me. After finding no openings as a bicycle mechanic in the local bicycle shop, it suddenly occurred to me that I could fix bicycles—on campus— perhaps in my dorm room. Five hundred half-page signs asking "Does your bike need repair?" plastered around campus soon had me spending a few days a week fixing bicycles in my dorm room. It was a great way to make money! A Saturday morning of tinkering with bicycles could easily net over $100—much more than one could earn through a work-study position. Plus, I was doing something I was interested in, having much fun, and making more money.

Upon relating my bicycle work to my sister, her first question focused on how my roommate felt about having bicycles and related components in our dorm room. My response was that all tools, components, and anything else related to bicycles stayed on my side of the room, and that my roommate was fine with how things were. Shortly thereafter she had an example for me. How would I feel if my roommate, who is a photographer, had cameras, tripods, and other equipment scattered about his side of the room? My response that I would not mind, that I would even be interested in learning how the equipment worked, did not satisfy her. She ordered me to remove anything related to bicycles out of the room and into the lounge.

This situation is an example of using typical logic on someone who processes things differently. It was only much later that I realized that it was possible that even though I would not mind photographic equipment scattered in the dorm room, like my bicycles, perhaps my roommate would have thought differently.

Towards the end of the school year my friend and I decided to part ways as roommates. Yet we remained friends, and still did things together at university, and we remain in contact to this day.

Academics

There was so much to choose from the buffet of fascinating courses at the university that I took more than the full-time load of 12 credits each semester, except for the last. The last semester was a student teaching internship, leaving no time to enroll in additional coursework. Although there was a wide diversity in how courses were structured and how professors taught, I was awestruck in that understanding course expectations was so much easier than in high school. Success in grade school seemed to depend on making educated guesses at teacher expectations, whereas at college level, I was amazed that my instructors clearly communicated their expectations of their students.

Perhaps maturation of my learning ability, differences in the way professors at college taught, or a combination of the two explain the sudden perceived change in how I processed course material. Whatever the case, it was certainly easier to determine and meet instructor expectations. I found psychology courses especially interesting because they helped explain to me the reasons behind human behavior that others seemed to intuitively understand. For example, when I became aware of the presence of body language, I conducted an empirical research project in the dining commons, examining the meaning behind why a student chose to sit at an empty table. Even to the present I am fascinated with books on non-verbal communication, such as those written by Alan Pease.

Professors who were structured in their delivery of information and content were the easiest for me to learn from. If structure was lacking, I was often successful in imposing my own sense of order on the course material. Once way of inserting structure was to take notes in a multilayered format, denoting levels of detail using different colors. For example, the main idea was in black, subtopics in red, divisions of those in green, and further prose-based explanations in light blue. The levels of indentation combined with the different colors helped me to map and retain key information for the class.

Courses lacking in structure, and where I was unable to impose an understandable semblance of order, were problematic. For example, I found it impossible to write a research paper for a physics of music honors section of a course because the only instructions given centered on the length of the paper, the number of references required, and the due date. At this time I realized that having intermediary deadlines would have resulted in successful completion of this assignment.

Graduate school

After graduating with my undergraduate degrees in music education and accounting and information, followed by a couple of years working, I returned to school for a Master's degree—and then a doctorate in music education—both at Boston University. Coursework for both degrees went reasonably well until I got to my comprehensive exams for the doctoral degree. While I felt reasonably prepared for the exams, there seemed to be unusual difficulty in addressing analysis of music from the Romantic era. In other words, music from other time periods from composers such as Vivaldi, Bach, Mozart, Beethoven, Debussy, Stravinsky, and others were fine, yet attempting to deconstruct composition from Chopin, Liszt, Wagner, and Brahms seemed to be an insurmountable challenge.

Appointments with a social worker eventually led to a full neuropsychological assessment, validating my suspicions that my childhood diagnosis of being on the autism spectrum was "haunting" me as an adult when processing relatively unstructured information—albeit in more subtle ways than when I was a child having difficulties in communication as a toddler—as well as social interaction and academics in grade school. Although recommendations for relatively mild accommodations were included on the report I shared with the music department, there was so little understanding about autism in higher education at that time that the music department and disabilities office did not know how to provide proper support.

For example, the director of the music department, who had dyslexia, believed that difficulties in processing music from the Romantic era could be overcome by merely repeating courses. Rather than advocating on my behalf, the director of the disabilities office told me a story about a person who did not receive accommodations because he was not substantially qualified for the job, suggesting that perhaps I was not properly qualified to earn a doctorate in music education.

Although I knew I had the Americans with Disabilities Act (ADA) on my side and winning a legal battle was possible, with learning more about autism and special education in general becoming rapidly more compelling, I felt it better to focus my efforts on "defecting" to special education. After much consideration and talking with people in a number of universities, I applied to Harvard University and Boston University Schools of Education. With my newfound knowledge about how autism affected me as a student, I made full disclosure of my history with autism, and submitted the then draft of my book, *Beyond the Wall: Personal Experiences with Autism and Asperger Syndrome*, as my writing sample.

Now involved in special education, I was curious as to what the disabilities office provided for college students with disabilities, and made an appointment to find out about what they did, rather than seek accommodations. It was a strange and somewhat tense meeting as I felt the counselors didn't quite know what to expect. Perhaps they were fearful that I would be angry about their lack of providing accommodations earlier and/or no student had previously asked questions about *what* they do in support of students in general, rather than asking for assistance for themselves. Numerous times I had to rebuff their offers to set up a file in case accommodations were needed. I declined as I felt I was able to self-accommodate for any learning needs that might occur in the doctoral program, but told them I would be back if I had any questions. Additionally, their lack of advocacy during my time of need while in the music program made me reluctant to have anything to do with them again.

With an acceptance from the School of Education at Boston University in hand, I started my program with a vengeance, taking two courses in the Summer session before I was to start in the Fall semester, with the full intention of completing the coursework in two years and finishing the dissertation in the third. Within those two years most of my coursework was completed, and I published the first edition of *Beyond the Wall: Personal Experiences with Autism and Asperger Syndrome*, and that's when invitations to present at autism conferences began.

Speaking at conferences was very rewarding. I met many others on the autism spectrum, their parents and other family members, educators, other professionals, publishers, and researchers in this field. Fortunately most of my coursework was done by this time, so I did not have to miss many class meetings. However, completing the comprehensive examinations and conducting my dissertation became challenging. I suppose writing two additional books along the way added to the distraction—until one day, my advisor firmly told me to stop writing books and to finish my work at the university. Until that time it almost felt that my career and involvement in the autism community was getting ahead of my doctoral degree, so it was good getting that dose of reality from my advisor.

Third time's a charm

A few years later, while speaking at a conference in Tennessee, the director of the disabilities office at Boston University emailed me, indicating that she had found the second edition of *Beyond the Wall* very interesting, and would I make an appointment for further discussion about it. The second edition described in detail my challenges in obtaining accommodations for the doctoral qualifier exams in music. While the names and the school remained anonymous, anyone involved in the process would be able to easily identify the people involved. A week later, she began our meeting apologizing for not providing sufficient advocacy in support of my request for accommodations in music due to her lack of knowledge of how autism may affect students in higher education. Her next sentence clarified her newly found interest in autism—her pre-school-aged son had just been diagnosed on the autism spectrum.

Realizing that people can make mistakes, and especially after apologizing for her errors, we became friends and presented at a number of conferences afterwards.

Threading the eye of the needle

In the Spring of 2008, while presenting at the annual Asperger Syndrome and High Functioning Autism Association Annual Conference, a woman who I perhaps faintly recognized hurriedly mentioned a faculty opening at Adelphi University, and encouraged me to apply. She recited her email address before slipping out the exit due to having a bad back.

Like many of us on the autism spectrum, my prosopagnosia makes it difficult for me to remember faces. However, a good friend of mine assured me that the person giving me this newsflash was a reputable person, and she had seen the two of us together in the past.

Having taught full-time in higher education during a former life as a professor of music, I understood how difficult it was to secure tenure-track professorship, and chalked up this potential opportunity as something to do for entertainment value as I went on trotting about the globe, consulting and talking about issues related to autism.

A few emails and phone calls later with this lady revealed a faculty vacancy in special education focusing on developing a graduate certificate in autism spectrum disorder studies—an area of special passion for me. Reluctantly, I went through the well-worn process of preparing my curriculum vitae, cover letter, and other application materials for yet one more job rejection. A few weeks later, I was surprised when the university scheduled an initial phone interview.

Having never interviewed on the phone, it felt like speaking to disembodied voices, with the speakerphone clipping off the initial hard consonants of words. Although those of us on the spectrum often have difficulty perceiving and decoding non-verbal communication, I found myself wishing for those cues telling me when it was time to stop answering a particular question, or nods of encouragement to continue speaking.

An invitation to a half-day on-campus interview quickly followed. Although there were some challenging questions related to education and autism, the very pleasant interview was missing a component that I have spent years talking about, honing, and providing recommendations around the world on—*disclosure about being on the autism spectrum*. My being on the spectrum was discussed, but in the much more pleasurable context of my work, and how having autism might be helpful in a university setting.

It was clear that the research the search committee members had done on my personal, professional, and practical background in preparation for our interview contributed positively to our conversation. The familiar and delicate tap dance moves those with autism and other conditions have to make (informing a prospective employer that one is different), followed by dropping pearls of wisdom as to why a person with that difference should be hired for the position, were just not needed.

However, the question of determining when it is appropriate to mention having autism is frequently discussed in the autism community. To me, it makes more sense to consider whether having autism significantly affects a situation or relationship, and there is a need for greater mutual understanding and support between the person on the autism spectrum and anyone else. If that's the case, then disclosure of having autism becomes a choice or option—often as part of a successful self-advocacy plan. For example, the chance of my disclosing that I'm on the spectrum to students in my computer class is much less than my telling people enrolled in my courses in special education and autism, because my having autism does not significantly affect my relationship with the students in my computer class.

Getting back to the interview, in researching my background, I was impressed that the search committee already knew my past and present relating to autism. After publishing three books and a DVD, writing articles, and traveling the world presenting and consulting on autism, any diligent search committee member would have found this out. Therefore, instead of working to convince the search committee of the benefits of hiring a faculty member with autism, we had a stimulating and meaningful conversation on what I saw as the future of people on the spectrum in areas such as education, employment, and the community.

The afternoon ended with the dean saying, "Well, you have a job if you want it." Five years later I remain joyful and grateful as a faculty member of special education at Adelphi University, just outside New York City.

Having now participated in a couple of faculty searches and co-chairing another, I realize that initial phone interviews are now commonplace. Here are some tips I have gathered to increase your odds of success when on the interviewee side of the phone for whatever job you may be applying for.

1. *Research the organization.* Be prepared to speak about:

   i. the organization's mission statement and how it relates to your personal goals. The interviewing department may also have a mission statement that should be worked into the discussion

   ii. how you plan to do your job within the organization.

2. *Prepare to talk about your working style.* One good way to do this is to imagine how a supervisor would evaluate your work. Or explain what a boss might see if they were to observe you on the job.

3. *Stand up when talking.* This improves breathing, and makes for a richer tone of voice.

4. *Prepare to be interrupted while giving your answers.* Although you may not have completed your response, the interviewers have heard enough of the answer for them to make a decision. If you feel you have not got to a vital part of your answer, ask toward the end of the interview if there's time for you to answer that interrupted response more completely.

5. *Make sure you have intelligent questions at the ready,* all pertaining to the specific position you applied for, when you're asked if you have any further questions. General questions about the organization are good to ask too.

6. *Above all, follow directions.* Provide the potential employer what they ask for, not more, and not less. Call the personnel office for clarification if needed.

As a bonus, preparing for these questions will help you be ready for the potential in-person interview should the organization continue to have an interest in your candidacy. Bring a copy of your résumé and cover letter in case they request it.

Some things to keep in mind for improving the probabilities of success include…

1. The interview begins the moment you meet the first person connected with the organization, whether it's the administrative assistant whose office you wait in before you meet the interviewer, or even an employee you greet when being taken for an office tour. All of these people may evaluate you formally or informally for mutual suitability.

2. As with the phone interview, you may be interrupted while giving a response. If this happens, just go on to the next question or topic of discussion.

3. Be prepared to talk about your previous relevant work experience, teaching style, strengths, and challenges using short responses that are no longer than a few minutes.

4. If a meal is involved, where you and the interviewer eat at a restaurant or in the building lunchroom, remember that this is still part of the interview. They want to see how you interact socially as a potential co-worker. Two helpful hints with the meal include:

    i. stay away from messy food such as pasta and sauce, or where the meal gets all over your hands, such as when eating lobster

    ii. avoid alcohol, even if the interviewer drinks and offers you the same.

5. Email a short thank-you letter within 24 hours after the interview. This letter can be used to emphasize a point you mentioned during the interview, or to bring something up not mentioned at the interview.

College from the other side of the desk

"These sure are talkative students!" was my first impression as I began teaching courses in autism and special education at Adelphi University after presenting internationally for over a decade. People liked my presentations, and often invited me to give additional talks, suggesting that I had presenting information to groups of people in the proverbial bag. Perhaps I did. However, things turned out to be very different when teaching in higher education.

--------------------------------- Takeaway

While there may be similarities between grade school or work and higher education, there are also going to be some large differences. It's important to be open to these changes in education, social interaction, and other aspects of being a college student.

My students seemed to engage in gratuitous social interaction that was so loud and garrulous that it almost hurt my ears! However, it was easy to get them to quiet down and for me to launch into a class session's worth of colorful PowerPoints, questions, and discussion. However, at times I had to derail inter-student discussion in order to finish the material I had for class. In order to improve my skills as an instructor, I knew I needed to seek support from my colleagues.

Part of being a professor at Adelphi University and most other higher education institutions involves obtaining and giving feedback to colleagues in a continuous quest to improve our teaching abilities. Doing so was initially very difficult because in a "previous life" as a professor of music, co-workers seemed eager to unearth nuggets of difficulty as a means for destructive criticism, making it impossible to remain at that school. A bit shell-shocked from that experience, I initially played it safe, and asked colleagues who I knew would give me friendly reviews before taking risks.

Takeaway

The adult world in higher education tends to be very different and more mature than in public school. Therefore it is easier to find people willing to help. Although bullying may be present, it is usually drastically reduced or just not present.

Ask for help from your professor, fellow students, a tutoring center, or a disabilities office. Make it your business to know where assistance can be obtained.

The written evaluations and following discussions generated from my colleague observations of my teaching were good, and I learned valuable teaching tips for the presentation of material and interchange of information between educator and student. However, I continued to be mystified by the "gratuitous social interaction" between students before, sometimes during, and after class.

Reaching out of my comfort zone, I asked a colleague with decades of experience as a special education teacher and administrator if she would observe my class. A straight shooter, she looked to me like someone who might tear you limb from limb, but fortunately I found her to be the total opposite. Her volley to my request was my objectives for her spending time in my classroom. Indicating that I wanted to improve my teaching, my colleague assented, and warned that it would be impossible for her to be silent in my class, and that she would join discussions and class activities. Her mode of blending in as one of the students helped me quickly forget that she was evaluating my teaching, and the session went well.

My colleague's feedback was fascinating. Her compliments on content knowledge, clear delivery, and beautiful PowerPoint slides were followed with an emphatic "Why do you chop off the discussions? Conversation between students are like pearls to be polished," she exclaimed. "It's clear you know how to present material. Now find out how the students feel about the material discussed. Find out about their impressions. Even ask them what they learned and if they found the session helpful."

Takeaway

You will learn a lot more going out of your comfort zone.

That may mean asking a question that you think everyone else knows the answer to. As I tell my students...the only stupid question...is the one you didn't ask because you thought it was a dumb thing to do. It's very likely that whatever question you have, others will have the same query—and be secretly relieved that you asked before they had to.

With a fresh set of proverbial ears I learned that inter-student conversation before, during, and after class usually focused on the course matter at hand, suggesting that didactically presenting material for the session covering the same ground through interactive discussion could be more beneficial and interesting for both students and the professor. Gradually, my teaching style morphed from talking with PowerPoint outlines to guiding student conversation to covered content. Teaching became easier, more rewarding, and even greater fun than before!

Takeaway

Be open to feedback as constructive criticism. You will learn a lot, things will make more sense, and life will become easier.

My changes in teaching style have morphed over into my presentations as well. While my talks—especially to larger groups—are more didactic, I enjoy engaging the audience in discussion where possible. Small groups often become workshop-like, with participant interaction and me coordinating a flow of information, concepts, and feelings rather than being the main focus of the event. Collaboration with the students as a facilitator rather than a didactic presenter was exactly what my college students and I needed.

Takeaway

My experiences as a professor in higher education were enhanced when I approached teaching course material in a collaborative fashion as a facilitator of acquiring knowledge. Similarly, it is the responsibility of the student to take an active role in their learning. Your return in higher education directly correlates to the effort you put into it. That goes for both students and their professors.

As a person on the autism spectrum, the lessons I have learned have important implications for individuals with autism making a successful transition into higher education and staying there:

» Just as you have preferred learning modalities, your professors are going to have particular teaching styles that are likely aligned with how they learn best. Your instructors may not even be aware that they are a visual, auditory, kinesthetic, or other type of learner.

» Adaptability is important. Whereas I began as a highly visually oriented instructor, I needed to work on auditory-based interaction with my students as well.

» Similarly, do your best to engage with how the instructor is teaching. For example, many times as a college student I would have to convert concepts presented orally into graphic form in order to make sense of the ideas.

» Listen to your mentors and others supporting you through college. Although it may be scary at times to seek and hear feedback, these people want to see you succeed, and will do what they can to make it happen.

4

Experiences of Individuals with Attention Deficit Hyperactivity Disorder

Francine Conway, Kelsey McLaughlin, Chanelle Tyler Best, and Sonia Minutella, Adelphi University and Derner Institute of Advanced Psychological Studies, New York

Overview of ADHD

Attention deficit hyperactivity disorder (ADHD) has been diagnosed in approximately 5.9 million children in the United States between the ages of 3 and 17 – 13.5 percent in boys and 5.4 per cent in girls (Bloom, Cohen, and Freeman 2012). Individuals with ADHD often have difficulty in more than one setting (e.g. home, school, work), and present with symptoms of inattention, hyperactivity, or both. Some of the symptoms of inattention include difficulties with sustaining attention or attending to details, completing tasks, following verbal and other instructions, maintaining organization, as well as an aversion to tasks requiring sustained mental effort, distractibility, and forgetfulness in daily activities. Some of the symptoms of hyperactivity or impulsivity include fidgeting behavior, difficulty remaining seated, excessive motor movement or speaking, interrupting, and intruding on others. The symptoms must be present for at least six months

(APA 2013). The prevalence of ADHD is such that students with this diagnosis have been identified as the second largest subgroup of college students with disabilities, with 4–5 percent of college students carrying this diagnosis (Harbour 2004).

Until 2013, the ADHD diagnosis was reserved for children who exhibited developmentally inappropriate symptoms of inattention and hyperactivity prior to age seven. However, with the revision in 2013 of *The Diagnostic Statistical Manual of Mental Disorders* (5th edition) (DSM-V), there is acknowledgement that the symptoms of ADHD persist into late adolescence and adulthood, resulting in an articulation of the parameters of the diagnosis that is relevant to these later developmental stages. According to DSM-V, for individuals aged 17 and older, five of the six ADHD symptoms must be present, and symptoms must be present prior to the age of 12. These changes in ADHD diagnosis have expanded the discourse of ADHD to its impact on individuals in the late adolescent and adult stages of development.

Given these recent changes in the expansion of the ADHD diagnosis to adults, it is not unusual for college students with learning challenges related to ADHD to be overlooked. Within college settings, it is extremely common for ADHD to be either misdiagnosed or missed altogether (Reilley 2005). Despite the universal acknowledgement that ADHD symptoms may persist throughout adulthood, minimal research focuses on ADHD among college students compared to research on ADHD among children and, more recently, among adults (Konold and Glutting 2008). Although, among the mental health field, it is widely accepted that ADHD leads students to experience disruptions in their academic pursuits and in their social adjustments to college life, the necessary accommodations and services that will better facilitate their transition to college life remain unknown (Norvilitis, Sun, and Zhang 2010).

Previously, up until the 1990s, it was widely accepted that symptoms present due to ADHD persisted throughout childhood. However, the hyperactive and impulsive symptoms are less apparent with the onset of adulthood, and those of inattention are sustained during adult years. In the late 1960s, the literature gradually began to introduce studies that confirmed symptoms of ADHD in adolescents, as well as adults (Okie 2006). In 1968, Harticollis reported on 15 adolescents and young adults who experienced behavioral symptoms such as impulsivity, hyperactivity, and aggression which extended throughout their adult years (Doyle 2004). In addition, in 1968, Quitkin and Klein studied 105 patients, some of whom were categorized into a group referred to as impulsive and destructive. Quitkin and Klein (1969) found that the patients with ADHD, within the impulsive and destructive categorization, displayed childhood histories of inattention, hyperactivity, and impulsivity (Doyle 2004). More recently, in a longitudinal study that followed children aged 6–12 for 10–25 years, 75 percent of the participants experienced the symptoms of ADHD into their adolescent and adulthood years (Weiss and Hechtman 1993).

The areas of dysfunction that may occur among college students include study skills, career decisions, and social adjustment. Unfortunately, the extent to which ADHD disrupts the college student's life does not cause a resonant shock throughout the mental health community. College students with ADHD experience severe lack of organizational skills, focus, attention, and academic coping strategies, which most often leads to procrastination and impairments in their academic functioning. In addition, they often fail to request the assistance of their professors, as well as other academic services, in anticipation of academic turmoil, worsening their academic functioning. Due to the debilitating impact of ADHD on the student's life, there is an immediate and urgent need, almost obligation, for colleges to provide guidance and assistance to these students (Turnock, Rosen, and Kaminski 1998). As colleges begin to properly identify students struggling with ADHD, retentions and dropout rates will subside, if proper services and accommodations are provided (Gerardi 1996).

It appears that ADHD diagnoses among the general adult population surpassed the ADHD diagnoses among the college student population (Wolf 2001). It is possible that these differences are due to the high dropout rate of students with ADHD or the avoidance of academic settings by individuals with ADHD. Those young individuals who attend college, despite their ADHD diagnosis, present a brave and persistent display of character strength. For example, students discussed using their creativity and mindfulness meditation practice to successfully and adequately persevere in achieving their learning goals.

However, those positive qualities that once resonated throughout their high school experiences subsided as their college years progressed. For example, those young adults with ADHD who attend college more frequently demonstrated academic competence during high school, compared to young adults with ADHD who do not attend college (Glutting *et al.* 2002). Young adults diagnosed with ADHD and attending college experience lower grade point averages (GPAs) and higher rates of under-achievement compared to other college students without the ADHD diagnosis (Heiligenstein *et al.* 1999). This dramatic shift in a student's performance in these markedly different settings can present a challenge for students who do not recognize the impact of the less structured college environment on their ability to function effectively. A student is then forced to recognize these differences and to seek assistance that may take some time as they try to resolve these differences on their own. College students with ADHD endure stress from contrasting sources, in comparison to young adults with ADHD who do not attend college, including academics, peers, parental supervision, and employment. Most notably, due to their attendance of college, they experience academic obstacles that may supersede other difficulties faced by individuals without ADHD (Konold and Glutting 2008). Students with ADHD have significantly lower graduation rates than their counterparts without ADHD. Approximately 5 percent of students with ADHD graduated from college, compared to 41 percent of students without ADHD (Barkley *et al.* 1990; Weiss and Hechtman 1993).

Difficulties in academic performance of college students diagnosed with ADHD

Academic performance is considered one of the most protrusive areas of dysfunction for individuals with ADHD. Past literature findings confirmed not only that those individuals with ADHD experience lower grades, higher rates of grade retention, and lower scores on standardized tests, but also that they exhibit frequent comorbidity among learning disorders (Frazier *et al.* 2007). Especially notable within the past two decades, difficulties among their academic performance continue past their childhood, obstructing their academic performance throughout high school and college (Frazier, Demarree, and Youngstrom 2004). Accordingly, young adults diagnosed with ADHD described a failure to focus, to meet deadlines, and to follow through on tasks perceived as insignificant (Murphy 2005). In addition, these students demonstrate diminutive time management skills and poor test-taking strategies (Reaser *et al.* 2007). Moreover, the subpopulation of young adults reported that they are less inclined to use problem-solving strategies to assist in planning (Young 2005). For example, a group of college students diagnosed with ADHD was assessed for memory and self-knowledge, and then compared to a control group of non-ADHD college students. The group consisting of the ADHD diagnoses recalled significantly fewer words in the self-referential condition, implicating that they lack a cohesive and organized personal narrative (Stanley, Cynthia, and Moshe 2011). The findings suggest that college students with ADHD experience complications in memory and planning, related to their executive functioning (Proctor and Prevatt 2009).

CASE STUDY EXAMPLES OF COLLEGE STUDENTS DIAGNOSED WITH ADHD

The following case study examples reflect the college experiences of a female and a male college student that mirrors some of the challenges ADHD college students encounter as depicted in the literature. Both students have had experiences with medication at different points in their lives, the male student as a child and the female student as an adult. However, their early experiences with school are mixed with both positive and negative learning experiences. A summary of their early experiences follows.

The female student was diagnosed when she was 30 years old. "I originally went to the doctor for a non-medical issue I was having and that was when it was determined that I had ADHD. I would forget important dates and people felt like I didn't care about things." After the diagnosis, she began taking medication to address her ADHD symptoms "I currently take Focalin and Vyvanse. They work for me... I feel the difference and see an improvement [in my concentration]." Although she described her early experience of school as mostly positive, she reported some mixed experiences. "It was really positive. I liked school but I had a tendency to lose my homework. Teachers were generally good to me. I only remember one teacher who seemed to not like me."

The male student was first diagnosed when he was eight years old. He reports that he has taken Ritalin and Adderall medications in the past, but is no longer on medication "I stopped my medication because I didn't like the way they made me feel. I didn't like the crash, or changes in my personality." His early childhood experience of school was mixed. As a young child, he reports "It was both difficult and fun at the same time. I was very hyper and easily distracted. Being hyper and loud at school was fun, and that was something my friends liked about me. However, in class I couldn't sit still, and I frequently had to take breaks from class time to go do other activities."

Academic experiences prior to college

Female student: "The transition was harder from elementary school to middle school because in middle school there was a different teacher every period and there was a lot of movement throughout the day, so I felt lost, both physically and mentally...in high school I continued to feel lost, I would catch up in the beginning and tell myself that I would do better this year, but then I would always fall behind, so I actually got pretty depressed by high school...my decision to go to college was mainly because my parents said you have to go to college, but I was so fed up of being in school, even though there were things that I did enjoy about it and had some accomplishments. I just didn't want to continue because it continually felt like a struggle and I didn't understand why, so I started to get depressed about it... I got a scholarship so my parents said you have to go, but the same thing continued to happen and I lost my scholarship. But after having to take an additional semester I did graduate."

Male student: "I didn't have great grades [in high school] so I had to do a post-grad year... I didn't think that I would be going to college but I did...it was a tough process, but I wanted to do it."

College selection

Female student: "Since my parents made it clear that I had to go to college even if I didn't want to, I made a deal with them where I would go and choose whatever major I wanted, so I chose something that interested me, which was music."

Male student: "I wanted to stay local, so I looked for colleges in my area...all decisions regarding college were made by me."

Female student: "I chose the college that I went to because they gave me a scholarship... I knew I wanted to go into a music program so that was a factor as well."

Male student: "I applied to colleges based on their reputation and location...out of all the colleges that accepted me, I ended up choosing the college that seemed to be the best."

College admission process

Female student: "I felt overwhelmed. They had different components like essay writing which was something I [had] struggled with since middle school, but when I finally submitted everything, they were pretty good...it was challenging because I worried about meeting the deadlines and getting everything that the college needed to them."

Male student: "It was a difficult, long process, but I managed to get through everything okay."

College life: first day of school

Female student: "It was great, I was very excited... I felt, like, here's another opportunity to get things right."

Male student: "Was an overall good experience and a good day, I can't think of anything negative about it."

Challenges on- and off-campus

Female student: "I would get involved with a lot of extracurricular activities and then my academics would slip. Planning was also hard, along with dedicating time to study... I was partying and drinking more when I got to college, so that definitely affected my schoolwork... I didn't have challenges in terms of roommates because I was a commuter."

Male student: "Staying focused in class was a challenge... I lived on-campus for my first year but I decided to move off-campus because I wanted more privacy and independence."

Experiences with professors and peers

Female student: "I felt like I had good interpersonal relationships with people...a professor once told me that I didn't respect people's time because I constantly got to her class late, and it really had me thinking because I never really thought of it, so it surprised me. I still got to class late after that, but I just felt really guilty about it."

Male student: "I had mostly positive experiences, but I knew that anything that affected me in class with professors was probably my fault…professors generally went out of their way to help me."

Support system

Female student: "My family has always been a great support system, but it was challenging to them because they knew I was smart and I could get things done that turned out great once I put my mind to it, but then I would fall behind in school and they would get frustrated trying to figure out why I couldn't do it…there was always a lot of encouragement and love, but I think my family eventually got a bit impatient… I felt like I always had people championing me, but they just didn't know what I needed."

Male student: "I can't think of any at school, but my family has always supported me."

Lessons learned from the college experience

Female student: "At the college level, the professors talk to you as an equal, an adult, so it helped me take myself more seriously… I met students from different parts of the world. They had completely different points of view for so many things which were really interesting to me, and it made it easier for me because I realized that people are different… When you realize that something is different about you, you learn how to accept it and you need to realize that it's a part of who you are and learn to live with it… I'm now able to see and understand several things at once, and I can juggle between things…do not be hard on yourself, guilt does not work, and ask questions."

Male student: "I learned to be independent and I enjoyed being independent...classes that appealed to me made it easier for me to do well in them...the amount of work that I had to do and staying on top of assignments made it difficult...things don't come as easy to me but that doesn't mean I'm not capable...if you take a long time to do something, that doesn't matter because you move at your own pace...don't give up, ask for help. I used to not care, but now I push myself."

Recommendations from college students diagnosed with ADHD

Female student: "ADHD screening sooner rather than later... I feel like ADHD is part of diversity [of the student body]."

Male student: "Extra time doesn't really help because having ADHD doesn't mean I need more time on a test. If I don't know the answers or I don't know what I'm doing, then that's the problem... I actually tend to be quick-minded... I think having teachers give more one-on-one time to students with ADHD would be a good thing."

Qualitative data of college students diagnosed with ADHD

We also included qualitative data obtained from an ongoing study investigating the difficulties experienced, within the academic, occupational, and social environments of college students diagnosed with ADHD. Rather than strictly evaluate the symptoms accompanied by a diagnosis of ADHD, we developed a self-report measure and focus group to explicate specific services and accommodations that participants confirm necessary for their academic, occupational, and social success within their present college. We utilized support groups to explore with students what learning difficulties they encounter, and to identify their learning needs.

Challenges within the college campus

Students expressed multiple challenges within the college campus, increasingly more so compared to those challenges that may present off-campus. Many students described an inability to sustain attentiveness, with a shortened attention span, and difficulty concentrating. Some acknowledged their likeliness to daydream and space out, completely abandoning their focus and their ability to follow through on tasks and activities. A female student stated: "Yeah, I see the professor talking in the front of the room, it's not like I'm not aware of that. But I'm also aware of a chip in the paint on the wall, and the person who dropped their pencil, and the branch bouncing a little outside the window... And even though I know I should just be paying attention to the one specific thing, I can't filter the other stuff out."

Some students disclosed their likelihood of experiencing panic attacks, while others described a persistent worrisome feeling due to their difficulties stemming from the ADHD diagnosis. Most interestingly, several participants explained their worry that other people would perceive them differently as a result of being aware of their diagnosis: "I feel as though people treat me differently when they discover my ADHD. They often look for me to do stereotypical ADHD things." Some participants disclosed their lack of organization, which often results in a failure to complete necessary tasks. In addition, participants reported a struggle with time management. A male student stated, "I can never sit down and do all my homework/work at once, which affects my time management negatively."

Services perceived as necessary by college students diagnosed with ADHD

When students were asked to identify those services and accommodations necessary to assist them in reaching their learning goals, many simply stated that universities failed to implement successful learning programs, expressing a devastated sense of hopelessness. However, they mentioned a desire for one-on-one academic assistance to facilitate their success within the academic setting, as well as scheduled meetings to complete necessary academic assignments and tasks. A male student stated, "I could go to the learning center so I can work with someone and be more focused." Lastly, students conveyed a wish for a solidarity group to unite a group of individuals diagnosed with ADHD to implement support and service throughout college. A female student stated, "[College] could have a club that does homework together and tries to eliminate distractions when doing work."

Learning experiences

Among the participants, a strong balance arose between those who categorized their learning experience as positive, and those who categorized it as negative. A male student stated, "The diagnoses strongly and negatively impact my learning abilities." Most students expressed a diminishment of their learning goals due to their ADHD. Another male student stated, "diminished learning goals, diagnosis has a negative impact on the learning experiences." However, those who categorized their learning experience as negative proceeded to do so because it presented yet another obstacle to overcome in order to accomplish those designated learning goals. Yet those same students expressed a sense of overall positivity while describing their college experience beyond the academic curriculum. Students frequently voiced a sense of gratitude for the services and accommodations that were in place to improve their transition into college, as well as a deep sense of pride when they accomplished specific learning goals thus far. A student exclaimed that, "I feel that when I get things done, my sense of accomplishment is more than others." In addition, those students who expressed positivity did so following the diagnosis, because those students had received the necessary medication, accommodations, and services. Therefore, they did not experience the symptoms of ADHD as positive, but the learning experience following the various treatments. A female student stated, "I take medication which has enhanced my learning." Moreover, students described alleviation through the diagnosis of ADHD and its implications. They frequently explained that the relief did not generate through the diagnosis, but rather through the services and tools the diagnosis provided to successfully reach their learning goals. In addition, several explained that the diagnosis was a relief because they no longer blamed themselves, believing that their academic difficulty was due to their lack of intelligence. A female student stated:

> And it was an immense relief... I had up until that point almost given up on school and learning entirely. Now finally, after all that time, someone is finally telling me that it's not my fault, and I'm not just an idiot destined to be a failure... Even more so, I think I started to do better because I finally had a reason to not just give up on myself. So the diagnosis improved my learning in so many ways I can't even describe. The ADHD hasn't changed at all, it's still there, it's just that having a diagnosis meant that I could finally start to deal with and cope with it. So definitely a positive impact on my learning experience.

Social support system

Students interviewed in the focus group described their networks of people who provided positive relationships through their interaction and communication as a method to cope with their diagnosis. A female student stated, "seeking support as well is a good way to cope with the diagnosis." Another female student stated "and socially, I don't really think it makes a difference. Which, likely is just because of the group of friends I surround myself with. They're all just as zaney as I am, so the extra energy and randomness fits in quite well around them. I got lucky like that." Most commonly, participants identified their friends as their source of support, especially those who experience similar learning obstacles, such as inattentiveness, distractibility, forgetfulness, and disorganization. A female student stated, "I hang around with students with similar interests and that are [as] competitive as myself." Some students attributed support to their families, especially prior to attending college. A female student stated, "I remember having anxiety attacks and crying to my mom at 3 am because I felt like I was sinking and I couldn't get out because my grades were dropping, and I felt incredibly overwhelmed with late assignments, and studying for exams I had in the morning or near future, and trying to keep up with my reading… My family is my best support system ever."

Comparison with peers

However, after the students' departure to college, their immediate access to their families discontinues, usually due to residence halls and leaving the family household for the first time. Therefore, it appears that college students rely on friends as their primary source for support, which can be beneficial, but also maladaptive, depending on the choice of friends. College students diagnosed with ADHD frequently compare themselves and their academic abilities with their peers. A female student stated, "I often felt as though I was not going to do as well as my peers." Although comparison with peers remains inevitable within the college environment, repetitive indications that their academic achievement may be less than that of their classmates may damage the student's sense of self. Continuous comparison with those peers surrounding the students may contribute to negative mental health outcomes, including low self-esteem. Another female student stated, "The diagnosis only really impacts my self-esteem when I'm having a particularly hard time with something other people find simple… I'll see that my friends in the class get it done no problem, but I can't do this simple thing that everyone else can do. Those are the only times where I really ever feel like I really have a 'disability.'" Much too often, students befriend other students who may not be aware of the implications of ADHD, and ridicule them for their behavior, whether it be innocent or not.

Recommendations

College students are required to assimilate into the academic, occupational, and social environment that is provided through the college institution. They must transition from a high school environment that provides numerous accommodations, support services, and structure to a college campus environment that provides significantly less support and structure. As a result, students entering college may experience higher academic-related distress and poorer academic performance (Heiligenstein *et al.* 1999). This transition phenomenon can be attributed to less structure inherent in college experiences and less parental supervision (Katz 1998; Parker and Boutelle 2009). Due to the public's stigma, students in need of support may be reluctant to seek help. Because students in college are now viewed as adults, they are required to independently seek out accommodations and support methods available on their college campus, and often fail to do so. Rather, they may fear being scrutinized or criticized, causing them to struggle without having their learning needs met. Therefore, more attention needs to be paid to the psychological adjustment of these college students to determine the necessary academic, occupational, and social support needed to ensure their success.

Pharmacological treatment

Stimulant medication and an extended release form of stimulant medication, as well as other psychotropic medications, have been used to treat young adults with ADHD—non-stimulants, antidepressants, and antiseizure medications. However, no double-blind placebo-controlled studies have been done with college students.

Educational treatment

Medication adherence is low in the adult with ADHD population due to the surrounding stigma of medication, in addition to the lack of surveillance within the adult population compared to the youth population. Therefore, there is a strong need for treatment strategies other than pharmacotherapy (Wentz, Nydén, and Krevers 2012). Individualized strategy instruction based on learning needs is recommended. Education interventions include one to three sessions for one to two hours each throughout the semester, or the use of assistive software programs for enhancing reading performance. When these interventions are implemented, students reported less fatigue and distraction, an enhanced reading rate, and less time to complete passages. However, these interventions do not lead to changes in reading comprehension. College students with ADHD may routinely need help with organizing assignments that are more global in nature. They can be encouraged to break tasks into smaller components of a simple structure, and to work through those individual segments. Students need help with routine tasks if they involve executive functioning, or they may need very specific, structured sessions when working with an academic advisor. Counselors, available through the office of disability services, might work with students to determine if they are able to make accurate self-analyses of their behavior by asking them to make a self-evaluation, and helping them consider the evidence for that conclusion. However, college students must request accommodations, which may or may not be granted. Along with the request, students must provide documentation by a professional (either a licensed psychologist, neuropsychologist, psychiatrist, or other trained medical doctors), dated within the previous three years. Moreover, the documentation must provide evidence of early impairment displayed in more than one setting, which may present a barrier to those students who have recently recognized the symptoms of ADHD and who have no previous history of the disorder. Academic accommodations comprise of extended time, a reader for exams, computer use for essay exams, a distraction-reduced environment, note-taking services, adaptive lab equipment and classroom technology, books in altered formats such as CDs or electronic books, tape records of classroom lectures, and preferential classroom seating.

Coaching

Coaching provides help to the student with ADHD in identifying important goals, and the plans and strategies required for achieving these goals. Coaching aids in monitoring progress towards these goals, identifying when the student may go off-track, and developing strategies to more effectively pursue goals over time. Coaching can help students develop their ability for effective self-regulation, and provide an important external source of regulation, as those abilities are developing. It has as its premise the ideology that people who are coached benefit from a holistic process that allows them to access their creativity (Hart, Blattner, and Leipsic 2001; Jaksa and Ratey 2006; Sleeper-Triplett 2010). Some researchers have explored the role of coaching as a tool for providing individuals who have ADHD with support and assistance with their organization and other executive functioning deficits. Coaching tends to be goal-oriented and a collaborative process that positions the client to be accountable for their goals (Parker and Boutelle 2009; Quinn, Ratey, and Maitland 2000; Whitworth *et al.* 2007).

Technology

In a pilot study by Wentz and colleagues (2012) using internet-based support and counseling, individuals received eight weeks of support via the internet (chat). Researchers found a significant increase in self-esteem after a six-month follow-up of their use of the coaching. In another study examining coaching students with ADHD, researchers found coaching had a positive effect on undergraduate students' executive functioning skills (Parker *et al.* 2013).

Disability and counseling services

Disability services provide accommodations to students including quiet test rooms, note-taker services, and skills training in time management skills (Quinn *et al.* 2000; Zwart and Kallemeyn 2001). Students may also benefit from individual and group psychotherapy offered by university counseling centers. In addition, some counseling centers provide psychiatric consultations regarding medication interventions (Heiligenstein et al. 1999; Weyandt and DuPaul 2006). Some students may be reluctant to disclose their ADHD diagnosis, although those receiving services during high school are more likely to disclose during college (Wagner et al. 2005). Considering the high dropout rate of high school children with ADHD, approximately 32 percent (Breslau et al. 2011), college students could also be at risk.

Future directions

Diagnosis of ADHD among college students and adults varies widely depending on the clinician's choice of self-report measures (Jackson and Farrugia 1997). However, due to the increasing opportunity for young adults to attend college, specifically those young adults pursing services and accommodations, additional diagnostic tools may prove useful throughout the diagnostic process (DuPaul et al. 2001). An individual's diagnosis of ADHD requires eligibility for services, according to Section 504 of the Rehabilitation Act of 1973 and the Americans with Disabilities Act of 1990 (Latham 1995; Richard 1995).

Despite the extended literature confirming that college students with ADHD are at great risk for academic impairment and under-achievement, minimal research has been conducted to examine the symptomatology of ADHD that college students experience (DuPaul et al. 2001). As a result, there is a scarcity of reliable and valid methods for diagnosis and treatment evaluation that further leads to an unawareness of the services and accommodations necessary for these individuals to succeed. Further research, utilizing reliable diagnostic tools rather than self-report measures, is required to determine the prevalence rate of ADHD within the college population, and to provide the appropriate services. Within the college campuses, students diagnosed with ADHD struggle to locate services that provide the necessary accommodations to assist them with their academic, occupational, and social needs (Javorsky and Gussin 1994).

Consequently, the prevalence of ADHD symptoms among college students will provide the necessary information to advance clinical research, intervention, and public policy.

Conclusion

In conclusion, ADHD originates during childhood, and for some may persist throughout adulthood. A growing number of longitudinal studies continue to support the existence of adult ADHD as the symptoms do not disappear, establishing it as a chronic disorder rather than an episodic disorder. Due to the recent changes within DSM-V, the expansion of the ADHD diagnosis to those individuals approaching adulthood prompted a further investigation of the learning challenges resulting from ADHD. College students, regarded as young adults, are required to assimilate into the academic, occupational, and social environment that is provided through the college institution. They must transition from a high school environment that provides relatively more accommodations, support services, and structure compared to a college campus environment. As college students, independence also means responsibility, as are required to seek out accommodations and services available on their college campus, which often presents difficulties due to the nature of their symptoms. Rather, the students may fear being scrutinized or criticized, causing them to struggle without having their learning needs met.

Previous studies demonstrate the significant achievement gap among those college students who suffer from ADHD and those who do not. Therefore, more attention needs to be paid to the psychological adjustment of these college students to determine the necessary academic, occupational, and social support needed to ensure their success. College students disclosed their desire to receive coaching in the form of one-on-one academic assistance and mandatory scheduling to complete academic tasks, as well as to be part of a solidarity group to foster social support. Perhaps additional studies designed to further extend the investigation of the accommodations and services they feel are necessary to improve their functioning within a college campus are necessary to ensure their implementation throughout college campuses. As awareness of learning difficulties and possible treatment and service options increases among the higher educational settings, the quality of education for students diagnosed with ADHD will improve. College students diagnosed with ADHD must persist and pursue their track of study to expand their opportunities and ensure success, especially because college settings enable students to declare their choice of study, and this encourages creativity and open-mindedness.

References

APA (American Psychiatric Association) (2013) *The Diagnostic and Statistical Manual of Mental Disorders* (5th edn) (DSM-5). Arlington, VA: American Psychiatric Publishing.

Barkley, R.A. (1990). *Attention Deficit-Hyperactivity Disorder: A Handbook for Diagnosis and Treatment.* New York, NY: Guilford Press.

Bloom, B., Cohen, R.A. and Freeman, G. (2012) *Summary Health Statistics for US Children: National Health Interview Survey, 2011.* Vital and Health Statistics, Series 10, No. 254. Washington, DC: US Department of Health and Human Services.

Breslau, J., Miller, E., Chung, W.-J.J. and Schweitzer, J.B. (2011) "Childhood and adolescent onset psychiatric disorders, substance use, and failure to graduate high school on time." *Journal of Psychiatric Research 45, 3,* 295–301.

Doyle, R. (2004) "The history of adult attention-deficit/hyperactivity disorder." *Psychiatric Clinics of North America 27, 2,* 203–214.

DuPaul, G.J., Schaughency, E.A., Weyandt, L.L., Tripp, G., *et al.* (2001) "Self-report of ADHD symptoms in university students: Cross-gender and cross-national prevalence." *Journal of Learning Disabilities 34, 4,* 370–379.

Frazier, T.W., Demarre, H.A., and Youngstrom, E.A. (2004) "A meta-analysis of intellectual and neuropsychological test performance in attention-deficit/hyperactivity disorder." *Neuropsychology 18,* 543–555.

Frazier, T.W., Youngstrom, E.A., Glutting, J.J., and Watkins, M.W. (2007) "ADHD and achievement: Meta-analysis of the child, adolescent, and adult literatures and a concomitant study with college students." *Journal of Learning Disabilities 40, 1,* 49–65.

Gerardi, S. (1996) *Factors which Influence Community College Graduation.* New York: NYC Technical College.

Glutting, J.J. Monaghan, M.C. Adams, W., and Sheslow, D. (2002) "Some psychometric properties of a system to measure ADHD among college students: Factor pattern, reliability, and one-year predictive validity." *Measurement and Evaluation in Counseling and Development 34,* 194–208.

Harbour, W.S. (2004) *The 2004 AHEAD Survey of Higher Education Disability Service Providers.* Waltham, MA: The Association on Higher Education and Disability.

Hart, V., Blattner, J., and Leipsic, S. (2001) "Coaching versus therapy: A perspective." *Consulting Psychology Journal: Practice and Research 53,* 4, 229–237.

Harticollis, P. (1968) "The syndrome of minimal brain dysfunction in young adult patients." *Bulletin of the Menninger Clinic 32,* 102–114.

Heiligenstein, E., Guenther, G., Levy, A., Savino, F., and Fulwiler, J. (1999) "Psychological and academic functioning in college students with attention deficit hyperactivity disorder." *Journal of American College Health 47,* 4, 181–185.

Jackson, B. and Farrugia, D. (1997) "Diagnosis and treatment of adults with attention deficit hyperactivity disorder." *Journal of Counseling and Development 75,* 4, 312–319.

Jaksa, P. and Ratey, N. (2006) *Therapy and ADD coaching: Similarities, Differences, and Collaboration.* Available at www.nancyratey.com/adhdcoaching/ therapy-addcoaching, retrieved on 8/11/2006.

Javorsky, J. and Gussin, B. (1994) "College students with attention deficit hyperactivity disorder: An overview and description of services." *Journal of College Student Development 35,* 170–177.

Katz, L.J. (1998) "Transitioning into college for the student with ADHD." *The ADHD Challenge 12,* 3–4.

Konold, T.R. and Glutting, J.J. (2008) "ADHD and method variance: A latent variable approach applied to a nationally representative sample of college freshmen." *Journal of Learning Disabilities 41,* 5, 405–416.

Latham, P.H. (1995) "Legal issues pertaining to the postsecondary student with ADD." *Journal of Postsecondary Education and Disability 11,* 53–61.

Murphy, K. (2005) "Psychosocial treatments for ADHD in teens and adults: A practice-friendly review." *Journal of Clinical Psychology 61,* 607–619.

Norvilitis, J.M., Sun, L., and Zhang, J. (2010) "ADHD symptomatology and adjustment to college in China and the United States." *Journal of Learning Disabilities 43,* 1, 86–94.

Okie, S. (2006) "ADHD in adults." *New England Journal of Medicine 354,* 2637–2641.

Parker, D.R. and Boutelle, K. (2009) "Executive function coaching for college students with learning disabilities and ADHD: A new approach for fostering self-determination." *Learning Disabilities Research & Practice 24,* 4, 204–215.

Parker, D.R., Hoffman, S.F., Sawilowsky, S., and Rolands, L. (2013) "Self-control in postsecondary settings: Students' perceptions of ADHD college coaching." *Journal of Attention Disorders 17,* 3, 215–232.

Proctor, B.E. and Prevatt, F. (2009) "Confirming the factor structure of Attention-Deficit/Hyperactivity disorder symptoms in college students using student and parent data." *Journal of Learning Disabilities 42*, 3, 250–259.

Quinn, P.O., Ratey, N.A., & Maitland, T.L. (2000) *Coaching College Students with ADHD: Issues and Answers.* Silver Spring, MD: Adventure Books.

Quitkin, F. and Klein, F. (1969) "Two behavioral syndromes in young adults related to possible minimal brain dysfunction." *Journal of Psychiatric Research 7*, 2, 131–142.

Reaser, A., Prevatt, F., Petscher, Y., and Proctor, B. (2007) "The learning and study strategies of college students with ADHD." *Psychology in the Schools 44*, 627–638.

Reilley, S.P. (2005) "Empirically informed attention-deficit/hyperactivity disorder evaluation of college students." *Journal of College Counseling 8*, 153–164.

Richard, M.M. (1995) "Pathways to success for the college student with ADD: Accommodations and preferred practice." *Journal of Postsecondary Education and Disability 11*, 16–30.

Sleeper-Triplett, J. (2010) *Empowering Youth with ADHD: Your Guide to Coaching Adolescents and Young Adults for Coaches, Parents, and Professionals.* Fort Lauderdale, FL: Specialty Press, Incorporated.

Stanley, B.K., Cynthia, E.G., and Moshe, L.L. (2011) "Memory and self-knowledge in young adults with ADHD." *Self and Identity 10*, 2, 213.

Turnock, P., Rosen, L.A., and Kaminski, P.L. (1998) "Differences in academic coping strategies of college students who self-report high and low symptoms of attention deficit hyperactivity disorder." *Journal of College Student Development 39*, 484–493.

Wagner, M., Newman, L., Cameto, R., Garza, N., and Levine, P. (2005) *After High School: A First Look at the Postschool Experience of Youth with Disabilities.* A Report from the National Longitudinal Transition Study-2 (NLTS2). Available at http://eric.ed.gov/ERICDocs/data/ericdocs2sql/content_storage_01/0000019b/80/27/fb/9d.pdf

Weiss, G. and Hechtman, L. (1993) *Hyperactive Children Grown Up: ADHD in Children, Adolescents, and Adults* (2nd edn). New York: Guilford.

Wentz, E., Nyden, A., and Krevers, B. (2012) "Development of an internet-based support and coaching model for adolescents and young adults with ADHD and autism spectrum disorders: A pilot study." *European Child & Adolescent Psychiatry 21*, 11, 611–622.

Weyandt, L. and DuPaul, G. (2006) "ADHD in college students." *Journal of Attention Disorders 10*, 1, 9–19.

Whitworth, L., Kimsey-House, K., Kimsey-House, H., and Sandahl, P. (2007) *Co-Active Leadership Coaching* (2nd edn). Mountain View, CA: Davies-Black Publishing.

Wolf, L.E. (2001) "College students with ADHD and other hidden disabilities: Outcomes and interventions." *Annals of The New York Academy of Sciences* *931*, 1, 385–395.

Young, S. (2005) "Coping strategies used by adults with ADHD." *Personality and Individual Differences 38*, 809–816.

Zwart, L.M. and Kallemeyn, L.M. (2001) "Peer-based coaching for college students with ADHD and learning disabilities." *Journal of Postsecondary Education and Disability 15*, 1, 1–15.

5

Voices of Individuals with Intellectual Disabilities

College—Do We Belong?

Karleen M. Haines, M.P.S.

My father always told me I can do anything I want
People with disabilities are doing things today no one imagined a few decades ago. They are protected by laws from those who may neglect or abuse them. They are provided with individualized support and treatment specific to their needs. They have jobs and friends. They are more integrated into social, residential, recreational, and community settings. Ultimately people who have disabilities have been looking to achieve some level of equality and satisfaction in their lives. Advocacy groups and non-profit support agencies, such as the United Way and the ARC of the United States (formerly the Association for Retarded Citizens), assist in pushing this agenda to society at large. Independence, the feeling of self-worth, and accomplishment, are important parts of any adult's life. For many adults, attending courses in higher education will widen their knowledge base, promote positive social interactions, and create a path towards a career and future financial growth. However, attending college can be difficult for adults with intellectual and developmental disabilities. The following highlights a few of the achievements

and barriers these individuals face, along with a brief history of those affected by this particular type of disability. The chapter ends with several case studies.

Many Americans will recall reading John Steinbeck's *Of Mice and Men* during their high school years, and becoming somewhat frightened by the character of Lennie, a killer with a sweet heart, who is big, simple, and easily persuaded. The story clearly shows that Lennie is slower than his companion George, and behaves in ways that he cannot control or sometimes fully comprehend. His impulses lead him to harm others without intent.

> Lennie went back and looked at the dead girl. The puppy lay close to her. Lennie picked it up. "I'll throw him away," he said. "It's bad enough like it is." (Steinbeck 1937, p.59)

In the United States, the history of how people with intellectual disabilities have been portrayed and treated is embarrassing, and in some instances, downright cruel. Carnivals, also known as sideshows or freak shows, traveling across country in the 19th and 20th centuries used some of these individuals for entertainment. It may be fair to say that the unknown and odd are often both scary and fascinating to most people. The fact that these types of shows became profitable business ventures for those willing to exploit individuals with limited capacity is not a surprise. There are many examples of people with disabilities who were under the employ of traveling shows. Joseph "John" Merrick, also known as the "Elephant Man," was a big attraction in the London area in the 1800s. Sam Torr, the owner of a local music hall, who was searching for oddities and novelty acts, discovered Merrick.

> An unusual human oddity is a showman's dream. Midgets, dwarfs, giants, and tattooed men are a shilling a dozen. (Drimmer 1985, p.68)

Merrick was put on display for patrons of the show in order to earn money. In 1886, to Merrick's delight, Sir Frederick Treves assisted him in his admission to the London Hospital for ongoing treatment. Medical professionals studied him with the hope of learning more about his deformities, and perhaps finding a cure. Surgeons, doctors, and the general public began to feel empathy for Mr. Merrick, and eventually those suffering from various forms of abnormalities. Around this time, "freak shows" became illegal in some parts of England and the welfare of the people being exploited became a human rights concern.

Natural order of things

Animals often kill or ignore the runts in their litter, perpetuating survival of the healthiest and strongest offspring in order to carry on their genes. This is a basic theory of natural selection. The central doctrine of evolution is the principle that those organisms that are better adapted to their environment "replace through competition the less well-adapted individuals of the species. This is the process Darwin called natural selection and Spencer called the survival of the fittest" (Montagu 1973, p.43).

Those born with genetic mutations and chromosomal abnormalities, such as Down's syndrome or Fragile X, have historically been seen as subhuman and as society's runts. It is interesting to consider that because an amniocentesis is legal, and often administered to pregnant women, it perpetuates the fact that a child found to have chromosomal abnormalities in utero should be considered for abortion. We are not lions in the wild. We are humans with higher levels of thinking, decision-making, and emotions. Opinions about the value of human life, particularly a disabled human life, vary because, unlike animals, we have the ability to hold spiritual, religious, and political beliefs. This causes us to ask questions such as: should a person with Down's syndrome be on a heart transplant list when a non-disabled person could benefit sooner? Should a disabled child be integrated into a classroom with non-disabled children, risking a drop in the quality of the teacher's lesson?

The quality and richness of curriculum for future special education teachers is important. A teacher's ability to understand his or her students as individuals, including their cultural and specific academic needs, is important. Parents of children without disabilities should be presented with the positive aspects of integrated school settings for all children. Though it is possible that a lesson will be impacted negatively by the presence of a disabled student in the classroom, there are ways of handling it. Depending on the child's needs, in-room support can be utilized in addition to the teacher's knowledge of, and commitment to, that special child's Individualized Education Program (IEP) goals. A student with special needs can also be pulled from the classroom for meetings with clinical staff, such as occupational or physical therapy.

The financial impact and the responsibility for cost of care are also true considerations. For example, programs in the USA, such as Medicaid and Medicare, support people with disabilities throughout their lifetime with everything from specialized education, habilitation therapies, medical care, to housing. Many states are fairly progressive in their policies regarding people with intellectual disabilities. There are many campaigns that seek to strike the "R-word" (retarded) from written documents and general vocabularies, citing the use of the word as highly discriminatory and hurtful. People with intellectual disabilities are a minority, not on the general radar of the larger community. Even in the USA, where there are parameters in place to assist these people with the right to be free from abuse, neglect, and discrimination, discrimination still occurs. Special victims units within law enforcement agencies continue to investigate crimes against these vulnerable citizens.

Moving away from institutions

De-institutionalization and inclusion practices began at the time of the Civil Rights movement in the USA. Care within institutional settings was poor, at best. Places like Willowbrook on New York's Staten Island were examples in the 1970s of the horrific treatment children and adults with this type of disability faced on a daily basis. These individuals were not treated like valued citizens. It was not common practice at this time to see a person with an intellectual disability as educable, a person who could benefit from training, live in an apartment, or attend college. We have come a long way since then, although there is still more to accomplish.

The field of developmental and intellectual disabilities is extremely diverse. It is important to understand the general categories of diagnosis. The following are several examples of diagnoses that may include an intellectual disability: Down's syndrome, Fragile X syndrome, autism spectrum disorder (ASD), pervasive developmental disorder (PDD), attention deficit hyperactivity disorder (ADHD), and traumatic brain injury (TBI). These diagnoses may be coupled with others that can be physical, such as a seizure disorder, cerebral palsy (CP), or blindness; or psychological, such as depression or bi-polar disorder. Causes range from genetic and chromosomal abnormalities, poor pre-natal care, exposure to toxins in utero, complications during the birthing process, and trauma to the brain.

The Diagnostic and Statistical Manual of Mental Disorders (5th edition) (DSM-V) defines the term intellectual disability:

> Deficits in adaptive functioning that result in failure to meet developmental and socio-cultural standards for personal independence and social responsibility. Without ongoing support, the adaptive deficits limit functioning in one or more activities of daily life, such as communication, social participation, and independent living, across multiple environments, such as home, school, work and community. (APA 2013, p.33)

Intellectual functioning also refers to intelligence. This is measured by an intelligence quotient (IQ) test. Those with IQ scores of 70 or lower show marked limitations and are considered to have an *intellectual disability* (ID), using the DSM-V current diagnostic term. This replaces the previous terminology of *mental retardation* (MR). Terms used to label and describe a person's clinical diagnosis have not always been considerate. Words that may have had meaning in a previous time can become obsolete or even derogatory. In this case, the term "retardation" or "retarded" is now considered to be culturally insensitive and outdated. The IQ score, along with other factors, determines the level of support required. A person with an ID will have some level of deficiency in adaptive behaviors. These are skills we use on an everyday basis, basic practical and social skills which include personal safety and communication, literacy and language competency, and financial responsibility and self-direction. An adult with a mild to moderate ID may not be able to read, causing major difficulties in researching bus routes to travel safely in the community, for example. They may have challenges in understanding the value of money, causing an inability to purchase just a few items at a store without full support. In more severe forms of ID, a person may experience the need for assistance with activities of daily living, requiring physical support in tasks such as dressing, utilizing a toilet, and brushing their teeth.

The basic range of categories, for an ID, based on IQ scores, is as follows: mild, 70–55, moderate, 55–40, severe, 40–25, and profound, 25 and under. People in the mild category show some marked differences in understanding social cues, and may need support in some tasks; in general they are more immature than expected for their age and have difficulty in regulating emotion. Those on the moderate level are behind their peers in conceptual skills and have difficulties in communication, displaying clear social limitations. Individuals with a severe level of ID are not often able to make responsible decisions regarding their wellbeing or the wellbeing of others; language and communication can be extremely difficult; and there may be maladaptive behaviors. A person with a profound ID is often non-verbal and dependent on care providers for basic activities of living, such as eating and bathing. Depending on their type of disability and accompanying symptoms, people with IDs may express themselves in abnormal ways, and have difficulty with communication and interpersonal relationships. They may display interfering behaviors such as self-injury, self-stimulation, or physical aggression towards others.

They can be susceptible to coercion, and can become victims of theft, physical abuse, bullying, ridicule, rape, or other sexual assault.

Legislation promotes a change for the better

An early diagnosis is helpful for parents and caregivers so that treatment can begin during an early intervention stage, or pre-kindergarten age. School districts are required by the Individuals with Disabilities Education Act (IDEA), originally enacted by Congress in 1975, to provide free, appropriate public education (FAPE) to all children regardless of their level of functioning. The passing of IDEA assisted in promoting inclusion and learning within the least restrictive environment (LRE). Each child diagnosed with an ID is provided with an IEP that tracks the student's progress and is tailored to his or her specific needs. Funding and access to necessary related services for children, such as speech pathology, psychological, and occupational therapy is also provided. Although outdated, some of the original language within the legislation was very clear on what Congress wished to accomplish:

> It is the purpose of this chapter to assure that all handicapped children have available to them...a free appropriate public education which emphasizes special education and related services designed to meet their unique needs, to assure that the rights of handicapped children and their parents or guardians are protected, to assist States and localities to provide for the education of all handicapped children, and to assess and assure the effectiveness of efforts to educate handicapped children (20 USC section 1400[c]). (Smith and Luckasson 1995, p.23)

The IDEA and the Americans with Disabilities Act (ADA) of 1990 helped children and adults with all types of disabilities by leveling the playing field, so to speak. The ADA legislated the right for those with disabilities, for example, to take a wheelchair onto a public bus in order to get to the grocery store, a college campus, or a place of employment. It mandated modification to things that the non-disabled population take for granted, such as curb cuts, graded sidewalks, closed captioning, the height of a sink in a restroom, and access to an elevator.

Special education

The IDEA includes transition services for older children and young adults, incorporating an individualized transition plan into the student's IEP. This is to specifically identify individual needs, post-school goals, outline action steps, and to coordinate resources. These plans focus not only on education and possible future employment, but also on other quality of adult life aspects such as residential living and recreation. In his ninth edition of *Exceptional Children: An Introduction to Special Education*, author William Heward summarizes the purpose of a transition plan:

> Beginning not later than the first IEP to be in effect when the child is 16, and updated annually thereafter—(a) appropriate measurable postsecondary goals based upon age appropriate transition assessments related to training, education, employment, and where appropriate, independent living skills; (b) the transition services (including courses of study) needed to assist the child in reaching those goals. (Heward 2009, p.570)

Options for young adults after high school can include post-secondary education, participation in some type of vocational skills training program, and supported employment. It is now a bit easier for a student with a mild ID to attend college. Even those with moderate IQ levels can attend some type of adult continuing education course. More colleges are offering courses that are tailored to this population of students, and the government offers various financial aid opportunities to pay for them.

The National High School Center at the American Institutes for Research indicates:

> The benefits of earning a post-secondary degree are clear, but minorities and persons with disabilities are disproportionately ill prepared to enroll and succeed in higher education. Fifteen percent of high school graduates with disabilities attend a four-year college after leaving high school as compared to 37% of young adults in the general population. (Yerhot 2012)

Options in employment

Work centers, previously termed "sheltered workshops," are large factory-type settings in which hundreds of adults with IDs work for subminimum wage pay. The US Department of Labor currently allows these supported settings, normally overseen by non-profit agencies, to pay a worker at a rate based specifically on their level of productivity, which is measured against the productivity performance of a person without a disability. For example, if a typical or non-disabled person is timed assembling 100 widgets in 60 minutes, and a person with a disability is timed producing only 40 widgets in 60 minutes, their productivity rate is determined to be 40 percent. Therefore, they would be paid only 40 percent of what a typical worker would make for that type of job. In most instances this is below the minimum wage rate. Adults with disabilities can be paid at rates as low as pennies per hour, based on these guidelines.

The federal government and state legislators are now pushing the agenda for fair wages for all adults, including those with disabilities, thus ending the subminimum wage allowance. This means that many sheltered workshops will close for good as their funding sources dry up, forcing many adults who have relied on these programs for employment to seek other options, however limited those options might be.

Supported employment programs offer some assistance in finding work by offering support staff members with a title such as "job coach" or "employment specialist." These staff may help the individual in several ways: do assessments to determine best job match, counsel individuals in various areas such as interview skills and proper work attire, train for travel skills on public transportation, shadow the person on-site after they get the job, be present in any supervisory meetings, and advocate with the manager on behalf of the individual if needed. Many of these coaches will job develop and canvas within local stores in order to find positions and managers who are actually willing to hire a person with a disability. Discrimination and ignorance are often a barrier. There are times when employers who are open become saturated with requests and may hire a handful of supported employees. The danger lies in the employer having one bad experience and, as a result, never wanting to hire a person with a disability in the future. Social Security Disability Insurance (SSDI) and Supplemental Security Income (SSI) are government programs providing money to children and adults with disabilities for various living expenses. These benefits can be adversely affected if a person maintains gainful employment and makes over a certain dollar amount in wages. People with disabilities and their families often therefore seek part-time employment. An additional barrier is high unemployment rates overall, causing adults with disabilities to compete for jobs with non-disabled jobseekers who may have degrees or better qualifications.

Not many adults with disabilities have any post-secondary education or degree. Because of this, those finding employment are consigned to working in entry-level positions with commensurately low wages. Sheltered workshops or large work centers do train many adults on factory-type work, such as picking and packing or sorting and assembling. Many special education programs in high schools seek to provide practical work experience by offering some on-site work-study and volunteer programs that expose the student to an actual employment setting. In general, adults with lower IQs are ill prepared to live the same life as people without disabilities. Many do not go away to college, drive a car, get married, have a full-time job, or move up the ladder in a company. This is not to say that these people are not living—what they feel is a full and satisfying life. It may just be a life that is different from the average person's life.

The following case studies share the stories of two people living with an ID and their experiences with education.

CASE STUDY: GIDEON

History

Gideon is a 25-year-old male of Haitian decent living with his parents. He has two older siblings and attended and completed high school on Long Island, New York. He is a very quiet young man and can often be shy. He is a dutiful son who is caring toward and close with his parents. He often assists his mother in various household tasks and prepares meals. Gideon enjoys going to religious services with his parents every weekend. English is primarily spoken in the home, along with Creole. At the time he was tested, he was diagnosed as having "moderate" mental retardation, with an IQ score of 54. Assessments administered include 13 subtests of the Wechsler Adult Intelligence Scale (WAIS, 3rd edition). His tests indicate that Gideon has issues with his working memory ability, specifically that he may experience significant difficulty in holding information to perform a specific task. When providing him with a directive, it benefits him to hear the information in chunks, as he has difficulty remembering a long list of instructions. For Gideon, the processing of complex information is more time-consuming. He may need several extra moments to understand what he has just been told or what he has read. His current instructor at the work center shares that his curiosity often takes over, and he can be found wandering around and quietly observing his surroundings, though he is easily redirected towards his original task with minimal effort. He can read well, though he has problems with math comprehension—he scored in the mid-range on the digit span subtest. The WAIS includes a verbal IQ test and a performance IQ test; the digit span is a subtest under the verbal portion and proposes indicating deficiencies in working memory. A digit span subtest presents numbers, then assesses for accuracy after requiring the tester to sequence, recall, and verbalize. Gideon's basic cognitive ability is in the low range of intellectual functioning, as measured by these tests.

Gideon is in general good health overall, and maintains regular visits to his doctor. He is able to attend to all of his own activities of daily living and personal hygiene. He has a somewhat unsteady gait, slightly dragging his left foot when walking. He is not able to fully extend the fingers of his left hand. He has marginal physical stamina, and may need to take short breaks if exerting himself for extended periods. He speaks with a slight lisp and stutters on occasion, though he is able to articulate his thoughts. At times he may require prompting to speak louder as he tends to be soft-spoken. He is near-sighted and wears glasses. Gideon dresses appropriately and neatly for his age. He is a sports fan and likes to watch wrestling and football on television. His favorite, however, is basketball, which he also follows and sometimes plays with friends.

Gideon's parents report that during junior high and high school, his favorite subject was reading, and his least favorite was math. He strives to do well and wants to succeed. He mainly attended special education courses, and was not fully integrated during all classes with peers of his age. He has always had several friends he likes to talk to on the phone, and utilizes his computer to keep in contact with them. Gideon was a diligent student during school, and always completed his homework without much prompting from his parents.

Gideon does not exhibit many interfering behaviors or patterns of action that may inhibit his success. He enjoys the camaraderie of others. There have been several instances of Gideon writing to and calling a friend or acquaintance excessively, causing the person to cut ties with him or asking him to stop. In one instance, Gideon contacted a fellow male peer in his program, by phone, in the evenings, over 20 times within the first week after gaining his telephone number. The other young man's parents had to engage Gideon's father, asking for help in monitoring his phone calls. This is a rare occurrence, and when counseled on the matter, he was able to appropriately tailor his behavior.

After completing high school at the age of 20, Gideon was enrolled in a day habilitation program with a non-profit service provider not far from his home. Activities within this program assisted in providing further community integration and an ability to interact with peers by volunteering at various locations in small groups with support staff. After speaking with the coordinator of his services, Gideon and his family requested a more stimulating program in which he could spend his day. He then enrolled in a vocational skills training program after volunteering for two years. His support staff at the vocational program share that he is a pleasure to work with, though he has a tendency to wander from his work area. It seems that he gets curious about what may be happening in a different area, and wants to observe what is going on. He is quiet but very polite, and seems to take pride in his tasks. He attended several courses at the local community college geared towards learners with special needs at his own request.

Personal story

Gideon is a handsome young man, short in stature, with a long, oval face and large eyes. He does not smile often, though gives you all of his attention, and often tilts his head as he is listening. He likes to read, and seemed very proud of that fact. Gideon shared that he enjoys being on his computer and uses social media accounts, such as Facebook, to talk to his friends.

In school he was in special education classes along with other students with disabilities. He liked his teachers, particularly Mrs. Raynor, his reading instructor. Gideon shared, "Mrs. Raynor, she was my favorite because she helped me to read better. She was so nice. She talked to my mom and dad and told them about me and how good I was doing." Socially, he had what he describes as "lots of friends" and attended two proms with two different young ladies as dates. Gideon expressed that at times other students who were not in his classes teased him. "They would yell sometimes and call me 'Special Ed'." He made this statement matter of factly, and did not seem to be overly bothered by the memory. Gideon shared that he lives with his parents and loves them a lot. He mentioned having one sister. He said that he would like to live somewhere else one day, but that he was happy with where he lives, and likes his room.

School experiences

During high school Gideon attended a program that brought students off-site to various community businesses in order to learn vocational skills. He recalled two different training assignments—a toy store at a very large and busy mall, as well as a restaurant where he helped in the kitchen. He did not remember discussing his plans after high school with his teachers or a counselor, though he said that he did tell his parents that he wanted a job. College was not something that he believed was an option. After graduating from high school, he entered a volunteer program, and is currently attending a vocational program on weekdays. At the vocational center he has been involved in various tasks that mostly include packaging and assembling. He receives a small wage for performing these tasks. He recently began working on a project that involves dismantling electronics such as laptops and modems. Gideon enjoys this very much because he likes to be busy and gets paid a better wage. He added that he contributes positively because he "recycles computers to help the earth."

A few years ago he saw a flyer on a corkboard at the center. The flyer was for several adult education courses being offered at the local community college two weekday evenings and on Saturdays. Gideon's father assisted him in enrolling in several of the classes over a few semesters. Gideon shared that his parents paid for the classes, and that his dad would drive him and pick him up. He preferred Saturdays because he was at the center for most of the day during the week, and several of his friends from the center were also on campus that day.

Gideon completed four classes over four semesters. He completed two computer courses, a reading course, as well as one on money management. He enjoyed the computer class and said he learned things that he did not already know, such as how to use the "F" or "function" keys at the top of the keyboard, and how to look up things up on the internet. The topics that he learned during the money management course were not skills that he was currently using. The instructors were "nice to us" he explained—he did not feel overwhelmed by any of the assignments, and felt that they were patient with him and his classmates.

From a social standpoint, he had already established a handful of friendships with classmates because he knew them from the vocational center. There were times that Gideon had to wait for his father to pick him up after class. He shared that he did not engage much with other students, disabled or not, while in the hallways of the building or while walking through the campus. "No one stopped to talk to me. I didn't stop them either. I just waited for my dad and maybe took a walk to see things." He felt that the students were very busy, using mobile devices, or listening to music with their headphones. He recalled waiting for the elevator after class one day, standing next to another student. The buttons did not light up and they had waited for quite some time for the doors to open. He asked the other person if they thought that the elevator was broken. The student looked at him for a few moments, shook his head, turned away, and went to the staircase. "I don't know why he did that. Maybe he could not wait. Right after he left the elevator came and I took it by myself."

Gideon is happy to work around computers in his program setting, but wants to get a competitive job placement in the community. He would like a "real job," as he puts it, where he is hired at an employer's outside of the vocational center. He feels that with a little help he can do it. Gideon said that he would like to get a driver's license and a car someday. A full-time job would help him to pay for his car and other things that he wants to buy, like food, clothes, music, and sneakers. Several times he mentioned going back to college because he likes to learn. Gideon planned to speak to his parents again about enrolling in more classes. He did not know what type of topics he would like to learn about, though he mentioned that his ideal job would be to work in an office setting. He would like to work at a computer and wear a suit.

CASE STUDY: BARBARA

History

Barbara was born in 1964 on Long Island, New York, into a two-parent household with two older siblings. She was diagnosed as having "mild mental retardation from birth." Barbara is reported to have been late with all of her developmental milestones, and first spoke at the age of two. During her school years she was given some extra support through special education, though she was mainstreamed through high school. She occasionally met with tutors either by herself or with a small group of her peers after school.

Barbara graduated from a high school in the Brooklyn, New York, area in 1984.

Several of Barbara's psychosocial evaluations state that during her childhood she was never told that she had a disability, and that at home, her family did not speak of it. Her older sister stated in one report that they never used the word "retarded" around her. Her sister felt that because of this, Barbara was not aware of her own limitations, and added that she did not have a strong bond with her growing up. It was her sister's opinion that had there been more discussion during Barbara's formative years about her level of disability, she might have received better formal treatment.

Barbara is a very friendly and outgoing person. She is very talkative and can laugh or giggle at any moment. She has a great sense of humor and understands sarcasm, often making a funny remark to put a smile on your face and laughs with you. Barbara likes to tell others that they brighten her day, and will often say to people, "You're the best. You're simply the best." She enjoys giving people she likes a "thumbs up" while winking and grinning. In the past she has utilized antidepression medication. She displays signs of anxiety, particularly when speaking to someone in a position of authority. She consistently seeks approval from her supervisor regarding her performance, and will make statements such as: "I am doing a good job, right?" Barbara's need for consistent validation of her good performance requires more patience and extra time from her supervisors. This was a factor in finding a good job fit for her and a placement where she could maintain a strong professional relationship with her manager. Turnover in supervisors is always a concern for her job coach, because working with someone who is understanding and open is key to Barbara's continued success.

Barbara is not married, does not have children, and is currently not dating. She expresses overall satisfaction in her current life situation in this regard. She has maintained several short-term relationships with male companions in the past.

Barbara shares that she has several friendships with people living local to her apartment, and friendships that have developed with co-workers over the past few years. She has good general health overall, and sees her doctor on a routine basis. She is fully capable of attending to her own activities of daily living and personal needs.

Barbara's IQ level determination varied over several exams, with an overall range of 68–80. This puts her in a high level of adaptive functioning and in the mild category of ID. Exams administered include the WAIS and Vineland II Adaptive Behavior Scales. In her most recent assessment, over the past ten years, she was able to score highly on a digit span subtest, that is, she could listen to up to a six-digit number and repeat back what she heard, in addition to being able to repeat the number backwards. Barbara can read well and has adequate knowledge of basic information such as cultural references and simple history and geography. She is able to cook, and has done well on several safety assessments that include her ability to travel in the community and relationships with strangers. Although she does not drive or have a license, she is fully capable of taking public transportation. She tends to be trusting, and her family reports that she is easily influenced by others. She has annual sessions with support staff on how to recognize abuse, including how and to whom to report it. Barbara has a limited sense of financial responsibility, though she is able to pay her bills with some assistance. Six years ago she moved into an agency-supported apartment. Prior to this she lived in a two-story home with her mom and sister's family, which included a brother-in-law and two nephews. Her father passed away about ten years ago, and her mother just before her move.

Barbara is currently employed part-time, and works as a kitchen services assistant. Prior to this she had two jobs in the retail industry, lasting several years, one within the local mall and another in a shopping center. Her job at the mall was on a full-time basis, gaining her a sense of pride and a good paycheck. She ended up leaving that job due to an inability, or possibly a lack of desire, to shift her hours as needed, and her social issues within the very busy store. In her current position as a kitchen assistant, her duties include preparing the dining area, setting up chairs, tending to the requests of diners as needed, serving as back up to the kitchen staff, and cleaning up the dining area, wiping down tables, sweeping the floor, and preparing the area for the following day. She is consistently well groomed and maintains proper attire for work. She has received training on customer service-related functions as well as cardiopulmonary resuscitation (CPR) and work safety measures. While performing her duties, Barbara is focused and task-oriented. On a weekly basis she shares with her support staff that she wishes to gain extra hours at work or a second job in order to make more money. She verbalizes her desire to always be professional, though she has had difficulty with balancing work–life issues at times. An example of this can be found in her conflicts with peers at work while experiencing relationship problems with her most recent boyfriend. During this time she would cry while she was attempting to perform her work duties, and would discuss openly why she was mad or sad. She was unable to work efficiently, and as a result was sent home by her supervisor on multiple occasions.

Personal story

Over a few interview sessions regarding her general outlook, employment history, and educational experiences, Barbara shared her own thoughts. She is very tall, with blonde hair and gray eyes. She has a high-pitched voice and often giggles while expressing herself. Growing up she had more mainstream rather than special education classes. She learned alongside her peers, and was good with math. Barbara received her diploma with her class. During high school she took vocational courses such as home economics, baking, fashion design, computers, and typing. She remembered spending a lot of time at the local library alone, looking at and reading magazines and books.

Barbara was embarrassed about her disability because she did not feel understood by many people. There was another student, a girl, who bullied her during high school. She recalled confronting her directly one day towards the end of her junior year. "I looked in her face. Told her to stop being so mean, that I was not going to take it anymore and that she had better back off! You know what? It worked. She never talked to me again. She never talked about me again. I got what I wanted because I spoke up. I fixed it myself." Barbara shared that she didn't plan the confrontation at all—she recalled seeing the girl's face twisted with anger, she suddenly got a pit in her stomach, and worked up the courage to blurt out the words right at that moment. When asked what she would change about her high school experience, she very plainly expressed that she wished that bullying was not allowed. She felt that back in the "80s" it was okay, not like today, where there is much more awareness about the dangers of allowing repeated abuse by peers. She wished that there had been more emotional support for her in school.

School experiences

Barbara's high school teachers were good to her, and she shared that most were supportive and patient. Towards the end of school she was not really encouraged to continue her education by attending college. Her teachers did not talk to her about what her plans were, and she did not remember if she had ever been assigned a guidance counselor. When asked if her family spoke to her about attending college, she said:

> No. Not that I remember. But my parents were there for me a lot. My father said things to pump me up, you know? He would nod his head and smile. He always said happy things. My father always told me that I could do anything

I want. He's gone now, you know? But I remember that. Thanks for making me remember that.

When she was 27, she decided to enroll in several courses at the local community college. She knew of some friends from high school who went away to school, far from home, friends who lived on their own without their parents. Barbara shared that she wished she could do that too. When she took the step to attend college, her main goal was to help her get a job. A job meant that she would have money and more independence.

Barbara enrolled in several "adult continuing education" classes. A staff member in an agency that was serving her at the time assisted her in enrolling in the classes. Her family paid her tuition. She recalls specifically taking classes that lasted only three semesters that focused around her gaining secretarial or office work. Her favorite course was data processing. Barbara is a good reader and had taken typing classes in high school years before. She said that she had some problems at the beginning. She did not know many people and felt shy about raising her hand or interrupting the instructor. "I didn't want to embarrass myself, you know? I didn't want to seem like a dope in front of the other students. People seemed nice for the most part, though. I would come early sometimes and find the teacher and ask her questions then." Barbara found the college classes interesting, and in the end earned a certificate from the community college. During the time she was in classes and around campus, she made a few friends, but not many. She took public transportation to and from school.

Work history

After getting the certificate, Barbara looked for work but did not find a job where she could use her new skills. "It is okay I guess. I've never worked in an office. I did learn something new and had fun doing it, so that is good." She shared that she did not know of, or participate in, any type of job placement through the college, and was surprised to hear that some schools offer that service.

Her subsequent job history included being a support aide to several senior citizens in a healthcare setting, a fitting room attendant at a retail store, as well as stacking shelves and being a cashier at a department store. Barbara has been a kitchen assistant for over five years and enjoys it very much. She feels the most supported in this current job. Barbara has a job coach who helped her to get the position originally, and who visits her on a regular basis to see how she is doing. When she has a hard time, the coach comes to speak to her and her supervisor together. On occasion Barbara will gossip about her peers or become involved in the personal status of her co-workers, some of whom also have an ID. At times her immaturity and inability to curb her verbalizations make it difficult to maintain strong relationships on a daily basis. Because of her friendly and easy-going demeanor, she will always be apologetic and reach out to her peers for resolution after the fact; however, she has difficulty in taking a proactive approach and avoiding those situations consistently. Barbara's coach will counsel her on these issues, though she continues to have trouble in this area. She mentioned speaking to her coach quite often, about getting more hours in order to be full-time in her current position. Barbara would also like to get a second job where she could do arts and crafts and other recreational activities.

Barbara feels that her current employer has provided her with the best training, better than she received in high school or college. Along with her co-workers she is required to regularly attend in-services about various topics such as how to assist diners with specific needs, following safety protocols, choking procedures, following eating guidelines, as well as team building. In addition, Barbara has a CPR certificate that she renews every two years from the American Heart Association. It is interesting to note that her job duties require her to assist other adults with developmental disabilities. She is adamant about how much she loves to help these people. She feels good knowing that she is able to, in her own words, "nurture them." At no point in any of the sessions did Barbara discuss her own disability specifically. She did speak briefly about special education and used the word "mainstreaming." It is clear that Barbara knows she has deficiencies but is not open to talking about it. She did not identify herself with the group of individuals she assists at work. She stated, "Everyone knows they are special."

Barbara is supported through Medicaid-funded programs in various aspects of her life. Luckily she has formal supports that provide her with a person-centered approach to services. She feels that the staff supporting her are there when she needs them, and involve her in decisions about her life, rather than just telling her what to do. There are a few things that Barbara wishes to change. She is very optimistic about the future. She would like to begin dating again, but after giggling loudly, said she felt comfortable being single and living in her own apartment where she has freedom. She definitely wants to earn more money. "I want to learn new things. I want to be creative. I would like to go back to college really. I want to establish myself. That's what everybody wants. And remember my father said I could do it too."

GIDEON AND BARBARA: WHAT THEIR EXPERIENCES TEACH US

Life for an adult with an ID can be tough. Gideon and Barbara express this in their own words. For those with higher IQ levels, it is probably even tougher. These people have a better understanding of what their deficiencies are. The commonly used phrase "ignorance is bliss" does not apply to them. In their attempt to live normal lives as their peers would, and to integrate fully, they are constantly confronted with the fact that they are different. They carry on—with the proper supports around them, they can reach successes both large and small.

Their experiences highlight several things:

- Elementary and high school teachers should be committed to understanding the specific needs of their special students in order to encourage them to reach their true potential and to find the internal motivation to do their best.

- Educators and administrators should be aware of the bullying of special needs students in all forms, and assist in the safety of those students, both physically and mentally.

- Teachers, administrators, counselors, and families should begin to recognize the potential in some students with "mild ID," and the possibility of them attending some type of higher education post high school. They should be knowledgeable on how to navigate systems of enrollment and financial aid.

- Administrators, instructors, and professors at college level must also be sensitive and educated on the needs of students with disabilities. They should provide an encouraging and supportive environment, again, in order to assist students in reaching their full potential.

References

APA (American Psychiatric Association) (2013) *The Diagnostic and Statistical Manual of Mental Disorders* (5th edn) (DSM-5). Arlington, VA: American Psychiatric Publishing.

Drimmer, F. (1985) *The Elephant Man*. New York: GP Putnam's Sons.

Heward, W. (2009) *Exceptional Children: An Introduction to Special Education* (9th edn). Upper Saddle River, NJ: Pearson.

Montagu, A. (1973) *Darwin: Competition and Cooperation*. Westport, CT: Greenwood Press.

Smith, D. and Luckasson, R. (1995) *Introduction to Special Education, Teaching in an Age of Challenge* (2nd edn). Needham Heights, MA: Allyn & Bacon.

Steinbeck, J. (1937) *Of Mice and Men*. London: Penguin Group.

Wechster, D. (1997) *WAIS-III: Administration and Scoring Manual, Wechster Adult Intelligence Scale, Third Edition*. San Antonio, TX: Psychological Corporation.

Yerhot, L. (2012) *High Schools in the US*. Quick Stats Fact Sheet. Washington, DC: National High School Center at the American Institutes for Research. Available at www.betterhighschools.org/documents/NHSC_FactSheet_HighSchoolsInUS2012.pdf

6

Experiences of Individuals with a Learning Disability

Anita W. Frey, Clinical Assistant Professor of Special Education, Adelphi University, New York

Learning disabilities

Current estimation indicates 3.4 percent of school-age children who receive special education services have learning disabilities (New York State Education Department 2011). This is a reduction in the number of students classified as learning disabled in previous years. The reason for the decrease is not known, but there are suppositions that Response to Intervention (RTI), which allows schools to provide support for students without formal classification, may be responsible, although there is not enough data to support that as a reason for a downward trend. "Learning disabled," however, remains the largest category within special education.

The definition of specific learning disabilities (Section 602), according to the US Department of Education (2004), is:

Section 602. Definitions

29. Specific learning disability

(A) In general. The term "specific learning disability" means a disorder in 1 or 2 more of the basic psychological processes involved in understanding or in using language, spoken or written, which disorder may manifest itself in the imperfect ability to listen, think, speak, read, write, spell, or do mathematical calculations...

(B) Disorders included. Such a term includes such conditions as perceptual disabilities, brain injury, minimal brain dysfunction, dyslexia, and developmental aphasia...

(C) Disorders not included. Such a term does not include a learning problem that is primarily the result of visual, hearing, or motor disabilities, of mental retardation, of emotional disturbance, or of environmental, cultural, or economic disadvantage.

This theoretical definition becomes operational when the Committee on Special Education (CSE) establishes the existence of a learning disability. This takes place when the CSE reviews all required documents submitted by state-qualified evaluators. Such evaluations must be valid and recent, and include an IQ (intelligence quotient) score, psychological evaluation, academic standardized evaluation, social history, medical evaluation, classroom teacher's evaluation, and any other professional evaluation. The CSE seeks to ensure that the picture of the student is clear and accurate. Parents are involved in the CSE procedure, and the CSE seeks this consent and asks for input. In the case of the two case studies that follow, the CSE asked for and received a speech and language evaluation and an evaluation by an occupational therapist as well as a physical therapist.

The purpose of this testing is to see if the student has a disabling condition.

Both of the subjects of this chapter were classified as having a learning disability as defined by New York State regulations. (These are based on federal regulations, but in New York State,

CSEs must follow state regulations as promulgated in Part 200 of the Commissioner's Regulations.)

Each young person presented in this chapter has a very similar profile.

CASE STUDY: GEORGE AND MATTHEW

I asked two young men if they would agree to be interviewed for a chapter to be published in a book. They readily agreed. I have known these young men since they were about four years old. George is now 23 and Matthew is 27. They went to school in the same district, but did not know each other. Both had a very similar background, and both lived in a comfortable middle-class community in a suburb of New York City. Each boy grew up in a professional, intact family, and each has a sister. In both families the grandparents had a strong influence. In George's family, his maternal grandfather, a professional man, lived with them; in Matthew's family, his grandparents lived nearby, and Matthew speaks of them with great respect and admiration. He said his grandmother always accepted him just as he was, and she thought everything would be fine.

When these men were boys, about two years old, they showed signs of delay in the area of speech. Their parents sought help and they received services through the mental health department.

There is one interesting difference between the two, however. George wanted to make sure that his real name was not used, he wanted the tape used to record his remarks returned to him, and he wanted to preview what was written for accuracy before publication.

Matthew, on the other hand, wanted his name used and was not concerned about confidentiality. He said he would be glad if anything that was written about him made a difference for another person. He is very proud that, with his disability, he has finished college, is working, and is engaged to be married. He said that he had had a big struggle with bullies, and feels that all the insults he bore made him the person he is today, and he is delighted to let everyone know it.

George

George was born prematurely and received services through the mental health department when he was about two. When he was about three years old he transitioned to the Committee on Pre-school Special Education (CPSE) in his public school district. George received services as a pre-school child and was classified as a child with a speech impairment. (The state had not yet introduced the classification of "child with a disability.") For this reason, George kept that classification when he entered public school.

When George finished nursery school, his parents selected a private elementary school for him. He attended from kindergarten through second grade, and was successful in that environment. He did not act out and was not disruptive. In general, he was appropriate in that placement. For third grade George transferred to the public school in his home district and was evaluated by the CSE. His classification was changed from a child with a speech impairment to a child with a learning disability. He was placed in a general education third grade, and received resource room services as well as speech services, occupational therapy, and a one-to-one aide. (I have no record of why the CSE recommended an aide before he had even entered school.)

Academically George did satisfactory work, but he needed a great deal of support in school and at home. He always seemed to be under stress. School was not easy for him, even though he did well academically.

In public school, George had poor social skills, which seemed to be exacerbated by his one-to-one aide. He didn't interact with his classmates. The aide was always by his side and this made George different in the eyes of his peers as well as his own self-evaluation. In his mother's opinion, the aide's presence caused many of these unintended consequences.

In middle school his school problems continued. He was neither a bully nor an aggressive student, but he was picked on. He was teased so much he could not attend to class instruction, and was so hyperactive that he was told to leave math class almost every day.

The locker room was a very difficult environment for George. When he graduated from elementary school to middle school, the physical education routine changed. In elementary school he wore his gym clothes to school. In middle school he had to change into his gym uniform in the boys' locker room. Because the teasing and bullying were so severe, I was concerned for his physical safety. I called the physical education teacher and asked that a safe place be provided for George. He was allowed to change in the coach's office. It was for his physical safety that this took place—there were not enough supervisors in the locker room to guarantee his safety.

The bullying was so unrelenting that the CSE agreed to place George in a more restrictive environment so that he could reach his potential. He was sent to a Board of Cooperative Education Service (BOCES) school for students who had special needs and could not function in a regular public school. The students in the school he attended all had at least an average IQ or above, and severe social needs. In his new environment George thrived. He was in a safe place so he could learn.

George passed all his New York State Regents exams, and was awarded a Regents diploma.

His parents selected a small private college near his home. It was a very unsatisfactory placement. George received little to no special help. It had been arranged during the admission process that George would receive help in class. For example, he was expected to get class notes prior to taking a test, but he received this material only at the last moment. This made it very difficult for him—he depended on the notes to do well. He was very anxious to succeed. George told me during this interview, "A security guard followed me around the campus on a scooter." George said, "He did this to make my life difficult." George was small for his age and felt he "stuck out" because of his size. In George's opinion one professor was a poor teacher and mean. He did not explain why the teacher was mean.

After one year he transferred to Adelphi University in Garden City, New York. Adelphi University is a small college with a special program designed to meet the specific needs of students who are capable of college work, but who need some special considerations. George had help selecting classes. His advisors were there to help, and they succeeded in meeting his needs. Counseling and tutoring were always available for him. If students wanted to self-identify that they had special needs, the professors would provide special consideration for them. When George needed to take a test, he could go to a special location and the test would be available. The time could be adjusted to meet George's needs. This was not a unique situation—the university planned for these students. George availed himself of all the services he needed. He wanted to do well, and he did.

George found an element of peace and safety in college. His grades were good; he joined the Hillel Club and the Psychology Club. He made friends. He is now involved in the Young Alumni Club and enjoys it very much. He made one very good friend who he still sees. He does not have a girlfriend.

George did say that all was not perfect at Adelphi University. He had some challenges. As a social work major, he was required to do internships. Some situations were very satisfactory, but one was difficult. As he reported to me, "I could do nothing right as far as the mentor was concerned." In his words, "one was very abusive and she did not think I should graduate." He did not want to discuss that person. But he survived! George graduated in four years and was off to work.

George has been employed for one year. He works as a paralegal in a law firm, in his own space, and on his own computer. He reported during this interview that he likes his work and thinks he might like to go to law school. (I'm sure George has the intellectual ability to complete law school if he chooses to attend.) At this time he has not researched law schools he may want to attend.

George would also like to have a girlfriend—that's a goal he has not yet reached. George never mentioned that he had ever had a girlfriend, and he never mentioned online dating. He talked about the Young Alumni Club that he had joined. He attends the activities they have on campus and enjoys them very much.

When I interviewed George he suggested that any information I wanted about when he was a boy I should get from his mother. He said he could not remember. I'm sure he was right—so much of his early childhood was difficult and painful.

Reflections and lessons learned

I want to take this time to tell the reader of my interaction with George at his Bar Mitzvah. He read from the Torah (Jewish written law) with no problem. He was a poised young man on the Bimah (raised platform). He conducted himself with confidence and decorum. He did very well. He made his family and himself proud.

At the party that followed the Bar Mitzvah, he was a perfect host. Again, he read his part at the blessing and breaking of the bread. He was respectful to his grandfather, his parents, his teachers, his sister, and friends and relatives. His address was excellent and he thanked everyone.

Then I saw another side of George. When the music started, George turned into a graceful dancer. I never would have expected this. He was marvelous. He knew all of the new dances, and the old as well. He loved to perform and he was great! I loved to see George enjoy himself so much. It seemed all his stress and tension disappeared.

I hope the *joie de vivre* that I saw that day continues to be part of George now that he is an adult.

Matthew

Matthew is 27 years old and was a full-term baby with no apparent problems at birth. However, he did not talk until he was three years old. His parents sought help and through the mental health department he was classified as a child who was "speech impaired." This was a very typical classification for small children who had developmental delays and who were not physically or sense-impaired.

Matthew attended a private pre-school program for children with speech and communication problems. When he was four-and-a-half years old and of age to attend public school, there were professional disagreements between the public school and the private pre-school program. His parents were very apprehensive that Matthew would not function in public school. Personnel at the public school had no reason to doubt that the public school was the most appropriate placement—the faculty were very well qualified and were highly experienced in the field of special education. The family reluctantly agreed to place Matthew in public school. Matthew attended a self-contained special class with about eight other children. He received speech and language services as well as occupational and physical therapy. The program also provided adaptive physical education.

Matthew entered school in September barely speaking. He had only about one or two expressive language words, but his receptive language was better.

Matthew was a big boy for his age, had a pleasant disposition, but very poor physical coordination. He seemed to enjoy school. He liked what he did, was cooperative, and apparently tried his best. That seemed to be the work ethic that he established as young as five years old, and that has continued until today.

Matthew's parents were still very apprehensive about his placement in public school. However, there was a remarkable occurrence that took place in October after he entered school. The class was going to decorate pumpkins for Halloween. Matthew got off the school bus, saw his mother, and said, "Buy me a pumpkin. Make Mrs. Q. happy." Needless to say, Matthew's parents no longer suffered anxiety about the placement. That was the first time he had put two sentences together. He was five years old.

When Matthew was in a self-contained class he did not seem to be bullied. By the end of elementary school, he was fully mainstreamed. He was able to do satisfactory work with resource room help. Socially, he was still very immature, and did not make friends.

The family moved to another community when Matthew was in sixth grade, which was junior high school in that district. In Matthew's words, he was "the new kid" and "kids ganged up." His social skills were very immature—he missed many social cues. Matthew talked about the times other students "jumped" him and chased him down the hall and how they attempted to "beat me up." Matthew explained, "Teachers looked the other way when the bullying took place and I got punished." On another occasion, Matthew reported, "A kid asked me what the definition of a friend was? I didn't understand or answer his question, and so the other kid said, 'I'll show you, I'm going to beat the crap out of you.'" Then he chased Matthew around the room.

There were no interventions for Matthew. He was most often blamed for running in the hall.

By the time he was in high school, the bullying and teasing he had experienced in middle school escalated. He suffered both physically and emotionally.

One student, on the first day of high school, called him an "SEI," which means a "special education idiot." On another occasion, another boy tried to steal his book. Matthew retaliated (he never explained what he did), but that boy never bothered him again.

One particular egregious incident happened in high school. A student grabbed Matthew's arm and put it in a doorjamb and squeezed it. School staff attempted to blame the victim, but through fact-finding and litigation, he received a cash settlement. Another incident in high school occurred when a student threatened to set Matthew on fire. He told Matthew that such a plan would go into effect at graduation. It did not happen, but I wonder how much Matthew worried on graduation day.

Academically Matthew's work continued to improve in this school. He was an honor student. He passed all his exams and earned a Regents diploma. A real accomplishment for a little boy who did not talk until after three years of age!

Matthew was off to college! As I wrote this chapter, I asked Matthew's parents when they began to encourage him to attend college. The answer surprised me. His father said that I had been the person who made them look at Matthew as a possible college candidate when he was very young. I'm not clear what was said particularly to his parents, but they remember. When Matthew was in second grade, I asked them how they saw their son 20 years from that date. At that time Matthew was making remarkable progress, but his parents saw more of what he could not do than what he could do. I, on the other hand, saw what he had done and was continuing to do. His father and mother began to think about goals.

When Matthew was in high school, I was invited to attend a CSE meeting at his school. The question of accommodations during Regents testing was discussed. Matthew's father insisted that he had to have a scribe. The teacher showed his father and the CSE Matthew's work. It was grade-level work, as the teacher had said. Finally, the father asked my opinion and I recommended that Matthew take the test without the scribe, as recommended by his teacher. Matthew passed the exam, and he did it by himself. His parents again saw what their son could do! I think college became much more than a dim dream—it was going to be a reality.

When Matthew was in high school he made the decision to attend college. He felt he needed college in order to pursue a career. He knew he would benefit from additional education. When Matthew finished high school his parents found there was a program at Adelphi University in Garden City, New York, for students who had a learning disability (the LD center), which suited him very well. The program at Adelphi provides tutoring, counseling, and a writing center. If students self-identify to a professor that they have a learning disability, they are entitled to take their exams in a special location and the time can be extended. Matthew took advantage of all that Adelphi had to offer. He received help from the LD center and said, "Many professors were very helpful."

College was Matthew's time to shine. He had friends; this was a new dimension in his life. He met a girl. As I write this, they are engaged to be married. They will marry as soon as Matthew has full-time employment.

Matthew learned a great deal from college. It was such a positive experience for him; he realized his own personal worth. He experienced growth, both intellectually and socially. He had friends, liked his studies, was well regarded by his professors, and he liked his teachers. Matthew seemed to grow up! He was ready to marry, find employment, and establish his own home.

After graduation (about five years ago), Matthew searched for a job. Aside from the fact that the job market was not good, Matthew had no specific, marketable skills.

Through a contact (after nearly five years' of job hunting) he got a part-time job in the public library in his community. He works about 35 hours every two weeks. He is a page in the library with "special rights." That job requires him to shelve books and help clients find books through an electronic tracking system, for which he received training at the library (hence, "special rights"). He can help out at the front desk, checking books in and out.

Matthew has now received his Civil Service documents. He took the Civil Service test and failed it, but by documenting that he has a disability, Civil Service granted a 55B waiver.

Now that he has all the necessary documentation, he is eligible for full-time employment in the public library system. Matthew has applied for another librarian position in another community and, as of this date, he has been offered a Civil Service job in that library. However, this position is also part time, but he will keep his original library job. He will have two part-time positions. Matthew is very satisfied with this arrangement, while he waits for a full-time position, because now he and his fiancée can set a date to be married.

Matthew believes that he should have additional library skills. He is thinking of going to graduate school for his Master's degree in library science. However, he is very aware of the financial and time demands of marriage. School at this time is a hope for the future.

Reflections and lessons learned

When asked about changes Matthew would make to the system, his immediate reply was more help from the college placement office and Vocational and Educational Services for Individuals with Disabilities (VESID). In his opinion, neither service was satisfactory. He had found his jobs through people who knew him and knew of job openings. Job placement should be better.

Matthew is very anxious to live away from his parents' home. He feels he wants to establish his own home, and that his parents should have their own time to live where they want and not be concerned about him.

Matthew has expressed that his family was always there to help. As far as college is concerned, he had difficulty being specific about what he had learned exactly, but he does know that the college environment made it possible to have friends, and most of all, he met his fiancée.

When the interview was just about over, the tape was turned off and we were chatting about the interview. Matthew said, "I knew when I finished college that I was not an idiot." I was very surprised by this remark. It didn't fit in the conversation—there had been no reference to the term. Matthew explained, "When I was in about fourth or fifth grade the teacher called me an idiot because I had made some mistake in the classroom." That remark had bothered him all these years. Each hurdle he crossed he told himself he wasn't an idiot. It was the last thing he wanted to talk about before we finished. He was about nine years old when a teacher made that remark. Eighteen years later he still feels the sting.

The future for George and Matthew

We can see that growth continues. Can we expect continued growth? Will George go to law school? Will Matthew receive a Master's degree in library science? Will both young men develop the social contacts that they find satisfying? Will they establish their own homes and their own families?

If I were asked any of these questions when these men were four years old, and compared them to other four-year-old children, I think my answer would have been slow in coming. The growth that these two men have made is remarkable. Is there room for continued growth? Are there still hurdles to get over? Clearly they have goals they have set for themselves, and all indications would point to "yes." If they could surmount the problems they encountered as very little boys, they should and could continue to grow and achieve.

I also wonder what kind of case history would evolve without so much parental support and encouragement, without school systems and colleges that addressed the needs of these young men. How often do well-intentioned, but poorly informed people ask if the tax money spent on children with academic problems is well spent? *Sit res ipsa loquitur.* Let the facts speak for themselves. Both men are employed in competitive jobs, with job skills that provide an income that will allow them to live independently, and with dignity. Could this have been the situation without support from family and society? I doubt it.

Learning disability is almost a mysterious handicap. It is sometimes obvious, sometimes hidden, and the definition is elusive. It is treatable, but not curable. People with learning disabilities can learn and work around their disability, but it is always "there." It may be "there" in obvious ways, in subtle ways, in painful ways.

These are case studies of two men who made excellent adjustments to adulthood, but underlying their successes are threads of pain. The recall of emotional, social, and physical pain is real. Family has helped, education has helped, but the underlying rejection by peers, the cruelty of bullies, and the meanness of teachers has not been forgotten.

Educators, child advocates, and parents can learn from the experience of these two young men who so generously shared their experiences with us. At times they were emotional experiences for these men as they relived so much pain. The reader may also feel some of the pain, but more than an emotional response is needed if the suffering of children, adolescents, and adults with special needs is to be alleviated. Schools, especially, must be more proactive so that students can study and learn in safety and in peace.

The law provides relief for those who have suffered discrimination. Until relief is sought and penalties are severe, only then will schools take the demands of federal regulations seriously. All stakeholders must be continually trained in their responsibilities. Limits of indemnification and personal financial penalties that can be leveled against school personnel must be part of all administrative training. Schools are places for students to learn responsibility. Now let's make them a place for all stakeholders to learn their responsibilities.

References

New York State Education Department (2011) *Regulations of the Commissioner of Education*. Albany, NY.

US Department of Education (2004) *Individuals with Disabilities Education Improvement Act of 2004*. Washington, DC: Office of Special Education Programs.

7

The Myth of Equal Opportunity

A Personal Perspective

Ehrin McHenry

Introduction

Whether we like to admit it or not, prejudice and discrimination are part of modern-day society. People with disabilities are frequent victims of these phenomena, which Simi Linton (1998) has come to refer to as "Handicapism." Society has certainly come a long way in this regard, as evidenced by such legislation as the Individuals with Disabilities Education Act and the Americans with Disabilities Act, but the fact remains that people with disabilities (whether that disability is developmental, physical, or mental) often find themselves at a disadvantage, not because of their actual disability, but because of other people's presumptions regarding what that disability says about them. While most of us in the helping profession (meaning, as defined in an online dictionary, professionals who nurture "the growth of or addresses the problems of a person's physical, psychological, intellectual, emotional or spiritual well-being") would not argue that fact, we might be harder pressed to admit that we can sometimes be among the worst offenders. Though our actions may not be as egregious as some that we have seen from others, the mere fact that we so often act on our prejudices about people with disabilities, when we hold ourselves out to be the very people who will fight the hardest to support them to attain equal opportunity in life, perhaps makes us more guilty than those whose actions we would be quick to criticize. What follows is a narrative of this author's experience, as a person with a disability working in the helping profession, that I hope will stimulate readers, especially those who are helping professionals, to frankly discuss the role that they have played in discrimination against people with disabilities, so that we may work toward change.

To begin with, I want to make it clear that I do not believe that we, as professionals, can rid ourselves of our prejudices about people with disabilities. I know that pre-judgment is a natural cognitive process that helps us bring order to the world; I only want to point out the common prejudices that I have noticed within the helping profession that have led to acts of discrimination to bring greater awareness to the issue. Second, I do not mean to imply that people with disabilities do not have their own biases about the issue. On the contrary, I fully acknowledge as much, and I know that I, too, have my biases. Therefore, I feel compelled to give readers some background about myself before beginning an in-depth discussion about the issue at hand. Readers are free to decide for themselves how much weight to give the opinions discussed herein, but please understand at the outset that I mean no offense to anyone, and that I am expressing these opinions (which are mine and mine alone) because I have been asked to do so by a former teacher and current mentor who has convinced me that they should be heard.

Personal background

My own disability is known as spastic quadriplegia, a subset of cerebral palsy. It has left me unable to walk without assistance, so I usually get around using a motorized wheelchair, and I have a limited range of motion in all my limbs. As a result, I have struggled to master the activities of daily living (e.g. I could not use the bathroom independently until my senior year in high school), many of which I am still unable to perform independently (e.g. putting on socks). Though I am lucky enough to be relatively intact cognitively, it does take me longer than my peers without disabilities to complete many cognitive tasks, and my extremely poor visual perceptual skills have made driving impossible (my exaggerated startle reflex has a hand in that as well). These difficulties mean that I have missed out on a lot of experiences that are typically a normal part of growing up. For example, I never spent time in another person's home without a caregiver because it would be difficult if I had to use the bathroom, a problem that persists to this day because the average home does not have a bathroom that includes handicap equipment (i.e., bars near the toilet so I can hold on and keep my balance).

However, it was not until I entered high school that I began to feel disconnected from my peers, and thus to resent my disability, which I deemed the primary cause of my social difficulties— because I had had to spend so much time focused on educational difficulties in previous years, I spent very little time with my peers in social settings. In order to survive, I convinced myself that I would be able to make friends when I got to college and my peers were more mature, and I focused almost exclusively on academics. I told myself that the people who would treat me like a child (I could literally hear their voice pitch change when they addressed me, as if they were speaking to an infant, or they would ask the people I was with questions about me rather than asking me) were simply stupid, though now I understand that these people were not stupid—they were simply acting under the assumption that by responding to me like that, they were meeting me at my level. It was a false and very demeaning assumption, but not one borne out of any negative intent; in fact, they likely thought that they were doing the right thing by meeting me at "my level." At the time, though, I told myself that things would be different when I entered college and people were smart enough to know to treat me like everyone else, and that if they thought I was struggling with something, an offer of assistance would be the only special treatment needed. Similarly, I believed that well-intentioned but demeaning actions by people who worked to support individuals with disabilities (e.g. coaches on my sports team for people with disabilities intentionally spreading their legs to allow a soccer ball that I had kicked to go into the net, or picking up a baseball that I had hit and throwing it further away to give the appearance that it had gone a greater distance) would end because those actions were done for the benefit of children, and I would be an adult.

Post-high school education

While in the protective environment of the classroom, it seemed as if I had been correct: both college and graduate school represented periods of tremendous academic and personal success. I studied psychology as an undergraduate student and was able to almost exclusively enroll in only those courses that interested me since my scores on several advanced placement (i.e., college level) exams in high school had allowed me to have already received credit for most of the core curriculum before I was officially a college student. As it always had, my studious nature made me a fast favorite among my professors, so being in classes was always a pleasant experience, as I received a lot of positive feedback regarding both my intellectual ability and certain personal attributes (e.g. empathetic understanding and genuineness) that I was assured would serve me well as a practicing psychologist. Moreover, I completed my undergraduate studies at a small liberal arts college where everyone was a commuter, so I did not feel as if I missed out on any peer bonding experiences that might have come from living in a dorm setting. For the first time I found myself a sought-out partner for group projects and I always had someone (and oftentimes more than one person) who wanted to sit with me in the cafeteria between classes. This latter change was perhaps the one that I cherished the most, as a large portion of my unstructured school time prior to college was spent either avoiding the cafeteria, because I knew I had no one to sit with, or sitting alone.

Furthermore, though I rarely required accommodations beyond extended test-taking time, a note-taker, and accessible seating, I feel it is important to mention that I always found my professors and other support staff (i.e., disability support services workers) to be more than willing to work with me to meet my needs. Such willingness was not surprising to me because I had generally experienced the same prior to college, with only a few exceptions, which I knew I would have to accept because not all people are going to be nice, regardless of whether my disability is an issue or not. However, I will also say that I felt much more respected once in college as someone who knew what I needed, and that I was capable of making my own decisions in terms of what offered services to use. Prior to attending college, no educational service provider elicited my opinion about what services I needed; I was simply told what I was entitled to, and frequently had to use the service whether I wanted to or not (e.g. in middle school I had to leave all classes five minutes early to avoid crowded hallways). As a college student, I was part of the decision-making process, which is perhaps most clearly illustrated in an art class I took in my freshman year of college.

To understand why this instance is so prominent to me, readers must first know that I always hated art class. Due to motor and perceptual difficulties, I was never able to produce anything near the quality that my peers could, and I knew that. As early as elementary school, I was mortified to have my artwork displayed in the hallways alongside my peers, and so the college art requirement was one that I dreaded. Thus, my academic advisor purposely placed me in a class where the art itself was not as important as the communication behind it, with a professor who I was assured would understand, and he most certainly did. I remember getting my first graded project back and being astonished to have earned an "A–." Perhaps having seen my nervousness when returning the grades, my professor talked to me privately, and told me that he knew that I had done my best, and that if I continued to do so, my grades would reflect that.

By the time the final project arrived, I had received the same grade on all of the projects thus far and, combined with the written exam and papers, I was earning an "A" in the class. The final project, however, was more complicated than the rest. I no longer remember the specific details, but there was tracing involved and multiple replications of the design that was likely to be very difficult for me and would take me a long time to complete. Recognizing these facts, my professor devised a way for me to complete the assignment using a computer program, and asked if I would prefer to do it that way. I thought about the offer, and asked if I could try to do the project as the rest of the class would, and switch to the computer program if the task was proving too difficult. The professor agreed, and in fact it turned out that I did do the project in the same way as everyone else; I just spent some extra time in the classroom to do it. Though it may not have looked as good as my peers' projects, I remember being very pleased with the final product, and it was the first time I had ever felt true pride in a piece of art that I had created.

Of course, that is not to say that my college experience was without difficulty. Despite my social inclusion on campus, I did not spend time with peers off-campus. Even when a peer and I would agree to do something together (e.g. see a movie), my calls to try and set the plan in motion would go unreturned and unmentioned during future on-campus interactions, and I did not have the self-confidence at the time to inquire as to the reason for these indirect rebuffs. There was also difficulty finding me an internship placement during my senior year and, though certainly no one ever said that I was being rejected on the basis of my disability, concerns for my "physical safety" were frequently cited. The professor in charge of coordinating internship placements for interested students (the class was an elective) openly admitted that this concern was a legally acceptable way of saying that those in charge did not want an intern with a disability, and I ended up completing my internship at a homeless shelter where I was only permitted to observe direct work with clients, and was tasked with clerical assignments when on my own. I did not find these difficulties particularly troubling, as I reasoned that change is always a gradual process, so things would continue to improve as I continued through my educational training.

On entry into graduate school, where I now specifically studied school psychology, it once again seemed as though I was correct. My academic success continued, and my peers now occasionally included me in off-campus social activities. Unfortunately, though, when I began my fieldwork experience, my social difficulty once again reared its ugly head. I found engaging with the staff at the schools where I completed my practicum and internship work problematic; I was somewhat fearful of interacting with staff members, and I frequently found my comments completely ignored when I got up the courage to do so. Of the four fieldwork placements I had during my graduate training, only one was an exception to this rule. At this one site, the staff were responsive to my comments, and engaged regularly in friendly conversation with me during lunch breaks and in between team meetings. Moreover, the staff treated me as if I was a competent professional. For example, when a teacher of one of my individual counseling cases started noticing behaviors in the student that she felt were linked to emotional distress, she came directly to me with them rather than going through my supervisor, which in my opinion showed great respect for my position as the student's service provider. (It turned out that this student, a second grader in a primary school, was experiencing anxiety about his move the next year to intermediate school, which he and I were then able to work through in our sessions.) Similarly, teachers would call on me to do push-in lessons or to monitor their classrooms for brief times if they had to be out of the room, and when a parent of one of my counseling cases called the school looking for strategies that she could use at home to help her son cope with his anger, I was asked to generate them.

However, sites in which I struggled socially were more common and therefore more prominent in my mind, and I interpreted these struggles solely as a consequence of personal deficit. Yes, I believed my disability played a role, but only in the sense that it was the reason that my social development was stunted; the real problem was that I was now a *weird* person with whom it was too difficult to connect, which of course meant that I could never be effective in any service-providing setting. Such a belief was absolutely devastating to me, as doing this kind of work had been the focus of my life, and to lose it would mean having wasted my life. Though I was able to mask this devastation while with students (and perhaps had I been more open to seeing myself in an optimistic light, I could have seen the positive reaction that the students had towards me at all my fieldwork sites as evidence that I could not be *that* weird), doing so took so much energy that I could not carry that mask through the rest of my everyday life, and it was very apparent to anyone else who knew me that I was extremely unhappy and losing faith in my own ability to have a worthwhile future.

Struggles in the workforce

This bleak outlook on my future became exponentially worse once I graduated from school and began my attempts to seek employment in my chosen field of study. Interviews have been very scarce; out of the minimum of 200 job applications that I have sent out since graduation, I have been granted approximately seven interviews (I say approximately, because it is nine if I count the multiple interviews I had for one job that I was ultimately not chosen for). I have also had what I consider to be some eye-opening experiences on a few of those interviews that further demonstrate society's discrimination against people with disabilities. For example, during one interview, applicants were required to fill out an application for employment, which was a paper-based application in which the provided spaces to write responses were much smaller than my large handwriting could accommodate. In the past, I have dealt with such applications (e.g. college honor society applications) by bringing them home with me where my mother could write my responses and I could type out any required essays, yet I was not permitted to do so here because it was apparently very important that the application be filled out before leaving the building, even though it was a first round interview and the decision about whom to hire was by no means immediate. Thus, I was not surprised at all that I was not called back for a second interview; my submitted paperwork was messy and did not make me seem intelligent, but my large handwriting has nothing to do with my ability as a school psychologist, and had I been permitted the accommodation of taking it home and bringing it back the next day (or even to type my responses on a computer), my large handwriting would not have counted against me.

For those readers who might be skeptical (e.g. maybe my application was not even looked at once I left that interview because my performance was not strong enough), I do grant that there are situations in which the above experience is not indicative of discrimination, though I believe that no such exceptions can be granted for these next two examples. In another interview, which was at an elementary school on Long Island, New York, I knew that I would not be hired for the position because the school had no elevator, and the only room that I would have been able to access as an employee would have been the gymnasium. To be clear, I do not feel that I should have been seriously considered for that particular position no matter the strength of my interview performance, as I do understand that it would have placed a tremendous hardship on that district to hire me given the situation (and the staff were as accommodating as they could be during the interview—they interviewed me in the gymnasium and brought in a table so that I would have a place to do my writing sample, and a very kind gym teacher sat and spoke with me while the interview committee finished their previous meeting and gathered themselves in the gymnasium), but the situation itself is clearly demonstrative of discrimination.

In order to fully appreciate the level of discrimination exercised in this third interview experience, which is beyond doubt the most deplorable example, I must first share the unique backstory of how it came about. I had gone to a presentation at my undergraduate institution on autism spectrum disorder

(ASD), which is an area of tremendous interest for me that I have experience with, and the presenter mentioned that the agency that she works for would be starting a new branch of services for this specific population. When I heard that, my thoughts went immediately to the fact that if the agency was starting a new branch of services, they would likely need to hire service providers with experience in this area. Ever prepared to grab onto any potential job opportunity, I had brought copies of my résumé with me to the presentation that I shared with this woman (along with a brief description of my relevant experience), and let her know how excited I would be to work for the agency. I followed up a few days later with a phone call to the woman, reminding her of our initial meeting, and asking for the opportunity to speak with her in greater depth about my experience and about potential job opportunities with the agency. I was then invited to a so-called "invitation-only recruitment event" that would include a job interview. I was beyond excited for the event, and thought for sure that it would result in a job. After all, when I first met the woman from the agency I was in my motorized wheelchair, so I reasoned that I would never have been invited to the recruitment event (which I never would have known about without the invitation, because it was not advertised on the agency website) if they had viewed my disability as a potential problem. I researched the agency beforehand, and came up with questions and comments about each type of service that my qualifications would enable me to provide. Additionally, I took great care when filling out the application that had been emailed to me, which was one that my mother recorded my answers for, and I typed the required essay, and I had never felt more confident as I did when I went through the agency doors on the day of the event.

In some respects, my optimism was called into question right away. For one thing, people were being asked if they had "had time to fill out the application" as they entered, and those who said that they had not were simply provided a blank one to complete. I felt that they should have been turned away because the applications were sent out two weeks prior to the event, and anyone who could not find the time to complete the application in that time obviously did not care enough about working for the agency to be granted a position. However, I did realize that my view on the subject might be unfairly imposing my definition of a good work ethic onto others, and I was only mildly annoyed by it. Similarly, when I was given a reading comprehension test that barely qualified as testing comprehension (i.e., one could easily answer the questions with word recognition skills because the answers were taken directly from the text, with no true comprehension or analysis required), I dismissed it as being non-indicative of potential opportunities for me. The test was provided by the receptionist at the agency that day and given to everyone who handed in an application before interviews took place. Though my educational attainment surely illustrated that my capabilities were far beyond such a thing, I recognized that it would be discriminatory to give the test to some applicants and not to others. Moreover, I reasoned that the agency could very well be recruiting for unskilled positions (one of the items on the application asked if the applicant had graduated from high school) that might warrant such a test as well as for a skilled position that required some education and training. I thought for sure that I would be given fair consideration for employment.

Unfortunately, I found out how wrong I was immediately on being brought into a back room for my "interview." The woman conducting the interview did not ask me a question to start, nor did she begin with the common, "Tell me about yourself and your experience." Instead, her first words to me were, "I just want to let you know that we are only hiring for positions that require physical lifting, so you're not going to be able to do that." I was admittedly taken aback and elected to ignore the comment, hoping that if I spoke about my education and experiences, this woman would see the value that I could bring to the agency. (I feel the need to note that, in my opinion, my disability could be construed as an advantage. This agency exclusively services young people with disabilities and their families, and I think it would be a good thing for them to see a person with a disability who is successful and who has been able to find gainful employment, not to mention that I might be able to relate to the clients in a way that an able-bodied peer might not, since I know what it means to be a person with a disability in today's society. However, this opinion represents my own bias that obviously many other people do not share.)

Sadly, my attempts to focus the interviewer on my professional abilities were unsuccessful. Though she wrote notes as I spoke, she did not have a single follow-up question about my training or experience, and appeared solely focused on my disability, as she did see fit to ask, "What accommodations do you require to work?" The only other questions she had for me were how I had heard about the agency and what I had seen when I visited the agency website, which is something I mentioned having done. When I told her about all the areas I had seen on the website that sparked my employment interest, she repeatedly insisted that there was nobody currently at the agency who could provide me with any information about those services because everyone there was only interviewing for the positions that required physical lifting (this position was termed a direct service provider, and as described to me, amounted to a babysitter who would entertain and care for children while their parents had respite). Similarly, when I asked about the autism services, for which the website said only "Coming Soon," I was told that the agency did not know exactly what services it would be providing, and that it would not be known until January or February (this "interview" occurred in September 2013), when that branch of the agency opened, but that my résumé and application would be kept on file for six months, so if there was an appropriate position, I would be called back for another interview (guess where I'm placing my money on that one?).

At the time, I resisted what was an incredible urge to point out to my interviewer the absurdity of what she was saying (i.e., how could the agency not know what autism services would be provided until *after* these services began to be implemented, and how can something even be called a recruitment event when *all* the staff can only provide information about a single and very specific position within the agency?), and I left that day feeling more defeated than ever. I also viewed the agency in an entirely different light. I doubt that the agency would see fit to employ me (there was a space on the application that I filled out asking that the agency send me text messages about future available positions, and I have not gotten a single such message), or any other person with a disability, in any meaningful capacity. Looking back on it, I believe I should have known better than to think otherwise, as I have seen the reality so many times. For example, another agency that provides vocational services to people with disabilities (not one at which I have sought either employment or assistance) has actually presented on what I consider ridiculous and depressing "success stories," such as the young man with an ASD who earned a college degree but who works as a part-time bag boy in the Stop & Shop supermarket. Such examples, in which a person with a disability has a menial job that he is overqualified for, being called successes, are, in my view, another clear example of how pervasive society's discrimination runs. Can anyone imagine a college graduate without a disability working as a part-time bag boy being deemed as having a successful employment outcome? No, but because this young man has a disability, such an outcome is celebrated (i.e., the underlying belief being that people with disabilities *cannot achieve* the same level of success as their non-disabled peers).

It is important to note that existing research seems to support the notion that my own struggles to find employment commensurate with my ability and training are not unique to me, but rather are phenomena in common with the general population of people with disabilities. For example, Wilton and Schuer (2006) wrote that employer explanations regarding the unsuitability of people with disabilities in service jobs (i.e., care work) "often had little to do with the essential functions of specific jobs," even though legislation in Ontario (where the research was done) requires employers to "identify the essential components of a specific job so that non-essential components might be reassigned to other workers in the interest of hiring a disabled person. As an example…a person hired as a computer salesperson could not be required to carry computers as an essential part of his/her job" (p.189). This research also demonstrated clear biases that effectively guaranteed discrimination against people with disabilities, such as the supermarket manager who stated that when conducting job interviews an applicant's walking speed affects whether he or she will be hired (p.190), or the man who opined that the restaurant business is well suited for individuals with disabilities because "there is a lot of stuff that is not…let's not put the word mindless but doesn't take a lot of thought like portioning control and rice portioning, pasta portioning things like that. It doesn't take a lot of effort to do but it gives them something to do" (p.191). Put another way, this man is stating that people with disabilities are only suited for jobs that do not require thought or effort. Another man asked, "If they're an accountant and they are bound to their wheelchair, couldn't they get a job as an accountant somewhere that is wheelchair accessible? I don't see what the problem would be" (p.190). While this man is at least kind enough to assume that someone with a disability might be capable of being an accountant, he fails to see the harm in such people automatically having a smaller pool of potential job placements because we have to be concerned with the physical layout of buildings.

It should be noted that in some respects I understand the development of such attitudes about the employability of people with disabilities, and do not view such discrimination as malicious. For one thing, as Imrie (1996) pointed out, the attempt to fully include people with disabilities into society is a relatively recent endeavor. Remember that the Individuals with Disabilities Education Act was enacted in 1975, and the Americans with Disabilities Act was not in place until 1990, meaning that people with disabilities have long been portrayed as "inferior, dependent and, by implication, of little or no value" (Imrie 1996, p.397). We have also consistently been portrayed as "the recipients, rather than ever the providers, of help and support" (p.399), and I know that such an embedded status quo is extremely difficult to overcome. Second, I fully acknowledge that there are significant legitimate concerns that employers can have regarding the employment of individuals with disabilities (i.e., they should be as competent and efficient as other workers), and believe that because of the increasingly litigious nature of society today, legislation such as the Americans with Disabilities Act might actually be more of a hindrance than a help in regards to ensuring that people with disabilities are provided with equal opportunity in the employment sector. For example, Falender, Collins, and Shafranske (2009) outlined the care that clinical supervisors must take in dealing with people who have disabilities to avoid legal risks. Personally, I know that I am not necessarily as efficient a worker as a peer without a disability (e.g. I take longer to type reports), but I have enough passion for my work and a sufficient work ethic to compensate for that by bringing work home with me without the expectation that this work will be paid for; I know that spending extra time on my work is a sacrifice that I have to make in order to do my job well. Unfortunately, not all people share that work ethic and might sue for overtime pay or if they were let go because they were not completing their work in a timely manner, and potential employees cannot know from an interview which category of work ethic a person has. Thus, it is easier for employers to hire people without disabilities rather than people with disabilities because there is not as much legal risk associated with firing a non-disabled person if the job performance is poor.

Despite all of this negativity, in my case my graduate school program director still had faith in me, and when he needed two former students to serve as group leaders in a therapeutic program in which I had received training as a graduate student, he called on me to be one of those people. This program piloted participant-led psychodynamically infused group therapy for adolescents and young adults on the higher functioning end of the autism spectrum. To be honest, in retrospect, the fact that this program was the first of its kind is in and of itself proof that those of us in the helping profession are perpetrators of discrimination against individuals with disabilities. Conventional wisdom has been that individuals on the autism spectrum cannot benefit from such group settings. They are too egocentric and socially disabled, we think, to engage with others or to form the connection with others that makes those groups successful. But what if, by assuming as much about these individuals, clinicians are stopping short of getting to know these clients on the deep level that we so often strive to know other clients, in the hope that this knowledge will help to put our clients on the path to self-discovery and positive behavioral change? And what if, given the proper chance, adolescents and young adults with an ASD could, in fact, find meaning in such a group experience? Especially given the fact that an impetus for these individuals continuing to receive treatment into their adolescent years is so often social dissatisfaction, albeit sometimes only on the part of a family member or loved one, it seems essential that clinicians get to know these clients in the same way they would a client whose diagnosis does not imply core social deficits. The fact that a program that opened in 2009 was the first to consider these questions speaks volumes.

Perhaps more importantly, I should note that I first began serving as a group leader in this program in January 2012, and it is still in operation today, over one-and-a-half years later. Within that time, I have cultivated very meaningful relationships with each member of the groups that I lead, and the participants have clearly benefited. The participants, who, as stated above, range in age from adolescence to young adulthood (current members are between 17–27 years of age), have reported benefits from their participation in the group. Namely, they have reported feeling a lot happier now than they did before they started in the program, and feeling as though they have friends. These sentiments have been echoed by some parents as well, who have said that their children have been in a variety of group programs since elementary school, but this program is the first that their children are eager to attend without any cajoling. Of course, I do not mean to imply that these participants are "cured" (that is, in fact, not the goal of the groups—instead, I work to help these group members to make sense of themselves in the world around them so that they can find a comfortable and personally meaningful niche within that world), or that groups are without their challenges; that is simply not so. But the issue of my own disability has never presented a problem for them, and it is not because they have not noticed. At times they express curiosity about it (e.g. they ask how I do certain things in light of my disability), but they have never expressed doubt about my competency because of it, nor has it been a factor that I have had to overcome in order to gain their trust. In the one incident in which one group member did make a derogatory statement about my disability, he apologized immediately, letting me know that it was not something he meant, and that he was very angry that day; these feelings then became a point of therapy, and his affect improved markedly by the end of the session.

I do not feel that this point can be emphasized enough, since this population is assumed to be particularly rejecting of those who are not like them and those who are different, and they accepted me despite my obvious differences. No doubt I had to work for that acceptance, but they gave me a chance to prove to them that I cared for them and would try to understand them. I did that, and they do not mind that I am different; they never did. What mattered was my presence, commitment, and the genuineness of my attempts to know them. The same principles have applied in my work in a college support program that primarily services this population, where my role focuses more heavily on educational support, and, in fact, the individuals I work with have frequently come to my defense in the face of insensitivity from others. In the aforementioned incident regarding the angry group member, the other group members acted to ensure that my feelings had not been hurt. Specifically, I was compared to a character that the participants love from the *X-Men* films who is in a wheelchair and who has very special powers, and one member placed a protective arm around my shoulder and expressed his disappointment with the angry group member for his comments. Thus, it seems to me that the service providers could stand to take a cue from their clients about equal opportunity and true acceptance.

I know I have taken a lot of cues from the members of the groups I lead. As much as these group members have benefited from what I give to them, I have benefited from what they give to me. Though my program director will tell you that I have a long way to go in terms of my self-confidence, and I will be the first to agree, I am starting to become more secure in myself, both as a person and as a professional. Yes, my disability does present many challenges to my professional success, but these challenges are almost exclusively logistical (e.g. transportation to and from work), and the content of what I do is not affected. Additionally, I am now able to look at my fieldwork experiences in a different light as well. It is likely that personal deficit was not a factor in my difficulties interacting with staff, because maybe I am not personally deficient. My anxiety certainly played a role (what role my disability had in creating my anxiety is something that I am sure can be debated), but I now know that able-bodied and very competent interns have also experienced being ignored by staff, so my personality cannot solely be to blame. Had I been able to hear that during my internship year things may have turned out differently for me there, and I am sure that those stories were there for me to listen to, as it was only after some personal growth undergone as a result of my experience as a group leader with these boys that I have been able to begin hearing them.

Resulting assessment

To be clear, I believe very strongly in the fact that people should earn their success, and people with disabilities should be no exception. Hence, it irks me to see people over-accommodate for people with disabilities, which I have seen over and over again in the educational setting. For example, one young man who I now work with in the college support program for students with disabilities had an accommodation during his senior year in high school specifying that he not receive any homework assignments. As should have been predictable, a consequence of that has been that this young man does practically no work outside of class and support meetings, and he will talk openly about being lazy. (I know some readers may be tempted to attribute this young man's laziness to executive dysfunction that is part of his disability, but I assure them that a complete case study would not support that conclusion, and that his executive dysfunction is thoroughly addressed in support meetings.) That this "accommodation" could coexist in a society where not all public buildings are accessible is mind-boggling!

Outcomes such as the one described above should come as no surprise to any service provider. After all, the vast majority of research into parenting styles demonstrates that the permissive style, characterized by a high degree of warmth with little to no discipline, correlates with poor achievement, poor social skills, and extreme self-involvement. These outcomes are in large part why most of us who work with children advocate for practices such as setting and consistently enforcing reasonable boundaries and scaffolding, which has been defined by Berk (2005) as a changing level of support provided throughout the course of a teaching session. Berk writes, "the adult adjusts the assistance provided to fit the child's current level of performance. As competence increases, the adult gradually and sensitively withdraws support, turning over responsibility to the child" (2005, p.330). We know that children who are not held accountable for their actions will most likely grow up expecting others to do for them, believing that they will get what they want out of life through minimal effort on their own part, and they will not have developed the necessary skills to do for themselves; in a sense these children will develop a form of learned helplessness that will greatly decrease their chances for success. Perhaps more importantly, we understand that such a developmental course does not mean that a person is inherently "bad," as it is quite a typical effect; who among us would want to work hard if we could garner the same rewards without the hardship?

People who know nothing of psychological research would likely be able to predict such outcomes as well if they took the time to consider it, as they are quite logical and go right along with common sense. The phenomenon is at the core of the decades-old children's book *If You Give a Mouse a Cookie* by Laura Numeroff (1985), in which a mouse who is given a cookie rather than taught how to get one himself continuously asks for additional items until he at last asks for another cookie, thereby starting the cycle all over again. As a society we know these things, yet so often with our young people, and especially our young people with disabilities, we seem to be finding it increasingly necessary to bend the rules for them so that they can "earn" rewards that they have not truly worked for. Hence the young man who did not have to do any homework. I cannot say for sure what led to the decision to allow this "accommodation," as I was in no way involved in the process, but I am rather certain that some sort of prejudice and/or discrimination regarding people with disabilities was at its root. Perhaps those people making the decision felt badly for this young man because he has a disability, and he did not *want* to do homework, so it was deemed that he would not be expected to. Perhaps it was also believed that he *could not* do homework, though given his intelligence and clear ability to do work when his current learning strategist (a service provider who helps with assignments) sets the expectation at the outset of each of their meetings that he will do work, any such belief was very likely borne out of unconscious prejudices about the incapability of people with disabilities. Perhaps, still, it was done out of fear that failure to grant such an "accommodation," and thus allow the young man's incomplete homework assignments to impact his grade achievement, would be interpreted by his parents as a violation of the laws that protect the educational rights of people with disabilities, and would therefore result in a costly lawsuit that was worth neither the time nor the money. (In this case, the parents' prejudice would be at play, as they would be assuming unwillingness on the part of the service providers to do what was fair for their son because he has a disability.) Such litigious fears are a legitimate concern and must be considered even when service providers are being asked to do something that they do not believe are in a student's best interest, as lawsuits can create long-term hardship, no matter the result, including, but not limited to, financial losses and damaged relationships with students' families. Regardless of the cause, though, the result is clear: this young man believes and acts as if his disability entitles him to laziness.

At the same time, in order to earn what is commensurate to their skill level, people with disabilities need to be given the same opportunities as typical individuals in both educational and non-educational settings. As a person with a disability who achieved the highest academic achievements in college and graduate school, yet has had only a handful of job interviews since graduating in 2011, and is only employed in any capacity because graduate school mentors have recognized my skill, I do not believe that that is happening. While it is clear that people with disabilities can be very successful following the completion of their education (Dr. Stephen Shore, one of the editors of this book, is proof), I believe that equal opportunity for individuals with disabilities is more often the exception rather than the rule. Moreover, I believe that the attitude of service providers (whether expressed via over-accommodation that leaves a person with a disability ill-prepared for "real world" work, or via an absence of consideration once the person with a disability reaches adulthood) has contributed greatly to the problem.

Conclusion

Finally, I want to emphasize without question that despite my increased confidence in my own professional and personal ability since the days of my internship, my fears about the future are still very present, and grow stronger with each passing day. In little more than two short years (in August of 2016), I will lose my certification as a New York State school psychologist because the certification is provisional, and I must have three years of full-time work in a school setting in order to earn permanent certification.

Though all hope is technically not yet lost because I can apply for an extension of my certification if I do get employment by its expiration and at this point, the loss of my certification is really an inevitable reality despite the fact that I will not give up applying for jobs. Interviews continue to elude me and become more difficult the more time passes with no opportunity to perform certain core functions of the job (e.g. psychoeducational evaluations, functional behavioral assessments, or Committee on Special Education (CSE) meetings) or to experience changes brought on by new legislation (e.g. the Dignity for All Students Act). It counts for nothing that I continue to attend workshops and other training on these things to keep myself as updated as possible because my younger competitors for jobs have actually experienced them. And once my certification is lost, the seven years that I have spent on post-high school education become worthless. No one can find gainful employment with a Bachelor's degree in psychology, and a Master's degree in school psychology is meaningless without certification.

So, in my view, my whole life will have been officially wasted in just over two years since I have been so focused on education and securing satisfactory and gainful employment. The thought is too painful to bear (so much so that I am crying as I type), and I have no idea how I will get through it. It is a pain that I would not wish on anyone, though I fear that if these trends of over-accommodation at the educational level and absence of genuine consideration for employment (which may, in fact, be justified by the continuation of the aforementioned trend if education does not provide people with disabilities the skills to be productive workers), that pain will only become a more common and crueler reality for subsequent generations of people with disabilities.

The few people with whom I have shared these deeply personal and painful beliefs have tried to suggest a so-called "plan B" for me, such as pursuing a Ph.D. or an entirely different but related degree, like social work or mental health counseling. Currently, the Ph.D. idea holds no appeal as it has been presented to me as a way to become a researcher or a professor, and I have no desire for either role to dominate my professional life (nor do I want to be in school for the length of time it requires, particularly because of my age). I want to primarily provide psychological services to clients; I do not want to primarily conduct studies, write articles, or teach academic material. Thus, while the idea of becoming a licensed social worker or mental health counselor does have an appeal, I do not know that I have the motivation to return to school at all. Though I have certainly enjoyed it in the past, a big part of my commitment to it and my zest for academic engagement was my belief that such engagement would ultimately allow me to fulfill my professional goals; given my experience now, that belief is eroded to the point of near non-existence. Without that belief, the idea of a return to the world of exams, research papers, and the like seems to be little more than a boring and time-consuming exercise in futility. Consequently, I cannot say that I have a "plan B," and may not have one until the loss of my certification forces me to pick something. As such, I return to my hope for this writing that I stated in the beginning: I implore readers, especially those of you in helping professions, to truly think about and frankly discuss the role that you have played in discrimination against people with disabilities, so that we, as a society, may work toward change.

Lastly, I feel it is important to note that despite my current situation, I cannot say that I regret my decision to attend college or graduate school. Had I chosen a different path, I would not have had the opportunity to meet the adolescents and young adults with whom I work today and from whom I can see that my life has meaning (though I do often wonder if I would be in a better position and happier today had I taken the opportunity offered to me in tenth grade to join a trade school program that had job placement services on graduation). Moreover, my undergraduate and graduate school experiences largely remain among some of the best and most treasured that I have had, and I do believe that there is a place for individuals with disabilities in the post-high school educational setting; we, as a society, just need to do our best to ensure that this world provides such students with the equal opportunity that was the initial impetus for their inclusion.

References

Berk, L.E. (2005) *Infants and Children*. Upper Saddle River, NJ: Pearson Education, Inc.

Falender, C.A., Collins, C.J., and Shafranske, E.P. (2009) "'Impairment' and performance issues in clinical supervision: After the 2008 ADA Amendment Act." *Training and Education in Professional Psychology 3*, 240–249.

Imrie, R. (1996) "Ableist geographies, disablist spaces: Towards a reconstruction of Golledge's 'Geography and the disabled.'" *Transactions of the Institute of British Geographers 21*, 397–403.

Linton, S. (1998) *Claiming Disability: Knowledge and Identity*. New York: New York University Press.

Numeroff, L. (1985) *If You Give a Mouse a Cookie*. New York: Harper & Row.

Unknown Author (2014) "Helping profession." 16 March Available at http://en.wiktionary.org/wiki/helping_profession

Wilton, R. and Schuer, S. (2006) "Towards socio-spatial inclusion? Disabled people, neoliberalism and the contemporary labour market." *The Royal Geographical Society 38*, 186–195.

8

Bridging the Gap Between High School and College

A Program for Students with Autism Spectrum Disorder at Adelphi University, The Bridges to Adelphi Program

Mitch Naglar, Director of the Bridges to Adelphi Program, Adelphi University, New York

The transition from high school to college is challenging for any student. Students entering college are faced with many new and stressful situations, such as increased academic demands and workloads, limited parental involvement, having to develop time management and organizational skills, social activities and peer events, navigating new interpersonal relationships, functioning within group dynamics and adjusting to a new level of independence, and the need for self-advocacy. For many, it may mean leaving home for the first time, sometimes far away, to embark on their most significant transition to adulthood.

According to *The Diagnostic and Statistical Manual of Mental Disorders* (5th edition) (DSM-V) (APA 2013, pp.50–59), the diagnostic criteria for autism spectrum disorder (ASD) include persistent deficits in social communication and social interactions, deficits in non-verbal communicative behaviors used for social interaction, and deficits in developing, maintaining, and understanding relationships. Individuals with ASD may also struggle with restricted, repetitive patterns of behavior, interests, or activities, stereotyped or repetitive motor movements, use of objects, or speech, insistence on sameness, and inflexible adherence to routines, or ritualized patterns or non-verbal behaviors, and highly restricted, fixated interests. Also, those with ASD may struggle with hyper- or hyporeactivity to sensory input, or unusual interests in sensory aspects of the environment. Because all of these issues can occur on a spectrum from mild to severe, it is likely that no two individuals will present with exactly the same problem set.

Recent research has reduced the 1 in 68 children estimation for ASD prevalence to 1 in 68 (CDC 2014). An increased public awareness of ASD has brought increases in research and services for individuals of all ages with ASD. As early intervention services have been found to help children from birth to three years old (36 months) learn important skills, increased availability of services in grades from kindergarten to twelfth grade have also helped children achieve greater academic success. These conditions have set the stage for increasing numbers of individuals with ASD to enroll in higher education institutions (Blumberg *et al.* 2013).

The challenges for college students with ASD include difficulties with social interactions, executive functioning, and sensory issues which create barriers to their success in academics, relationships, employment, and involvement in the community (Nagler and Shore 2013). In particular, the first semester in college is a critical transitional period for students on the autism spectrum (Vanbergeijk, Klin, and Volkmar 2008). College students with ASD may struggle, often more than neurotypical students, with transitional issues such as getting from class to class in different buildings, safely navigating the new campus, managing long-range projects, accessing academic accommodations, and understanding the social culture of the campus.

Bridges to Adelphi Program

Based on principles of cognitive behavioral therapy (CBT) (Beck *et al.* 1979), person-centered therapy (Rogers 1961), and social learning theory (Bandura 1977), the Bridges to Adelphi Program (BAP) at Adelphi University in Garden City, New York, is designed as a multifaceted support program for Adelphi students who self-disclose with ASD or other non-verbal learning disorders. At this time, there is no separate application, documentation, or criteria necessary for students to enroll in BAP. If they are accepted to the university, and they believe that the services that BAP offers could be helpful, they can choose to enroll in the program without going through a separate application process. There is, however, a separate fee for BAP services.

As suggested by Vanbergeijk *et al.* (2008), BAP offers individualized and flexible, comprehensive, academic, social, and vocational services. Using a problem-solving approach, BAP services include help with executive functioning dysfunction, writing, test preparation, assignment completion, and social skills development (Nagler and Shore 2013).

Academic services

The primary academic services that BAP offers are provided by current Adelphi graduate students who are studying psychology, social work, education, special education, or speech and language theory. Staff work cooperatively, and communicate regularly, to identify the thinking, working, and learning styles, and struggles, of each BAP student in order to empower each student to cope the most effectively with his or her unique set of challenges.

In their research, Trembath *et al.* (2012) found that for young adults with ASD, their most common strategy for living and coping with anxiety was withdrawing from anxiety-inducing situations. Denial, avoidance, and procrastination are commonly-seen forms of these responses for college students with ASD to academic anxieties or fears of failure. Because these strategies can often result in academic problems, including failure, BAP staff regularly monitor for these responses, and focus on concrete strategies that encourage students to become aware of the ways that they deal with their academic anxieties, and they collaborate with them to try to identify different, more effective, strategies.

Because many individuals with ASD need help with organizational strategies (Adreon and Durocher 2007), and organizational help is critical to the success of a student on the autism spectrum (Vanbergeijk *et al.* 2008), each BAP student is scheduled for two meetings per week with an *academic coach*. The primary role of academic coaches is to help students stay aware and up-to-date with their current and upcoming assignments, available academic accommodations, and other scheduled meetings. At each academic coaching meeting students review the syllabus for each class they are taking, and with their coach create a concrete, concise, and clear report about upcoming assignments, presentations, exams, and meetings. In some cases academic coaches and students create detailed daily/hourly schedules. These can include schoolwork, on-campus appointments, meal times, study times, and designated times for sleep and waking. The clear and concrete design of these schedules are designed to help remind students what they need to do, and when they plan to do it, and as such they are helpful for the student.

Academic coaches also work with students on personal care issues such as developing strategies to learn to monitor and control when they go to sleep, and how to ensure that they will wake up at the appropriate time for them to get to classes and meetings on time. As their parents often provided such support and reminders for them prior to college, these are common areas of difficulty for students with ASD living on campus. Also, students with ASD who live on campus can often struggle with medication management and personal care issues, such as showering and/or wearing clean clothes regularly, because their parents often monitored these issues while they were living at home.

At the end of each academic coaching meeting, students receive a hard copy and an emailed copy of this schedule. Students are also asked to report on their progress on assignments and projects from previous meetings.

Each BAP student is also scheduled for two weekly meetings with a *learning strategist*, whose primary goal is to focus on assignment completion, research, editing of papers, or studying for the exams that the academic coach has documented. The learning strategist receives an emailed copy of the same report that the academic coach emails to the BAP student, and so is aware of the student's upcoming (or past due) assignments and exams. The student is encouraged to prioritize upcoming assignments, and to work on anything that is on the academic coach's list during meetings with the learning strategist.

While academic coaches are interested in how their students think about things, and use a concrete, concise, and clear approach, learning strategists are more interested in how their students learn, work, and process information. In order to best help their students, it is important for them to determine whether each student is a visual or auditory learner, or a creative, verbal, or pattern thinker (Wellkowitz and Baker 2005, as cited in Adreon and Durocher).

As no two students approach their schoolwork in the same way, learning strategists are encouraged to be more creative and flexible. Using a trial and error approach, learning strategists experiment with strategies and regularly make adjustments. For some students, large assignments may need to be broken down into manageable units, and explicit instructions for time management and scheduling of work may need to be suggested (Vanbergeijk et al. 2008). For others, improving study skills may need to be the primary area of focus.

Some strategies that learning strategists have found to be effective are "chunking," or breaking down large assignments into smaller steps (which reduces anxiety), reading assignments to students (with auditory learners), using flash cards to study for exams (with visual learners), and scribing for students, documenting thoughts and ideas while the student speaks them to help with written assignments.

Social services

As Adreon and Durocher (2007) note in their article "Evaluating the college transition needs of individuals with high-function autism spectrum disorders," "Perhaps the most challenging area for students with ASD is adjusting to the social demands of the college setting" (Welkowitz and Baker 2005), and they know that they lack the skills to master the most basic interactions (Glennon 2001), which may cause anxiety (Tremblath *et al.* 2012). For students with ASD, who may simply be trying to "fit in," these thoughts may be devastating. Therefore, having a positive social support system is important (Glennon 2001). In order to address the issues of social anxiety, stress, and avoidance, BAP uses a multifaceted approach, offering a setting and services that are designed to create the positive and safe social environment that Glennon refers to, to challenge the negative thinking styles that are common to individuals with ASD, and to provide a positive and non-judgmental social support system.

Because having a space that feels safe and welcoming to the students is important, both academically and socially (Nagler 2012), BAP office space is designed as a safe and available environment. There are individual, private offices that are used for academic meetings, and a central "hang out" area for students to congregate and socialize. The office is open, and staffed, from 8am–8pm Mondays through Fridays, and 9am–4pm on Saturdays. As well as staff members providing scheduled academic coaching and learning strategist meetings, there is always at least one graduate student scheduled to be available to BAP students for advice or study help.

Students are encouraged to spend their free time in the office, which they often do. Common activities are studying, playing video games, and socializing with other BAP students or staff members. For those with sensory issues, the office can be a place to eat meals in a quieter setting than the university cafeterias. Staff are trained to refer, or bring students experiencing extreme emotions, to the student counseling center for more serious or emergency situations.

Two evenings a week there are social group meetings that are led by graduate staff, which are open to all BAP students. Students are encouraged to attend these meetings in order to have opportunities to socialize with other BAP students, or to engage in group activities such as board games, video games, or to watch a movie. At some meetings, graduate students make presentations and lead discussions on topics such as emotional regulation and affect control, reading social cues, and the dangers of social media. If a student, or students, wishes to engage in a group discussion on a specific topic of interest or concern, staff will offer to moderate those discussions.

BAP also offers separate men's and women's groups, which are also led by graduate staff. These meetings are more structured, and most often psycho-educational events. Students are encouraged to express questions and thoughts that they would not express in co-educational group meetings. Issues discussed are developmentally appropriate for college students, such as dating and relationships, safe sex, online dating, and how to tell if someone is romantically interested in someone else.

Group outings and activities are also offered every month. Bowling, pool, dinner outings, and trips to Dave & Busters restaurants have been group favorites. The university provides transportation, so that students, staff, and peer mentors can travel together. Also, one time each semester, a "BAP video game night" is set up in a large meeting room on campus. At these events, multiple video gaming systems are set up, and students spend the evening gaming and eating pizza.

Adreon and Durocher (2007) state that the use of other, neurotypical students as mentors can be a useful support service for ASD college students. All BAP students are offered the opportunity to meet with *peer mentors*. These volunteers, who are undergraduate members of the Adelphi student body, receive training and supervision that provide them with guidelines and feedback for working with college students with ASD. They are asked to meet with their BAP student weekly, with the goals of "modeling appropriate social behaviors" (Bandura 1977), and to encourage and assist their BAP student to engage in campus organizations, clubs, and activities. When peer mentors have attended BAP social events, student attendance has increased.

Over the years, the relationships that have developed have been mutually beneficial. As a direct result of peer mentoring relationships, BAP students have had opportunities such as practicing with the university lacrosse team, painting scenery for university theater productions, and taking part in campus fundraising activities. BAP students have been receptive to this service because the peer mentors provide acceptance through unconditional positive regard, empathy, and genuineness. These relationships also challenge BAP students' negative predictions of social failure.

The Bridges research team designed a satisfaction survey to assess peer mentor satisfaction with their BAP experience. Responses found that 95 percent of peer mentors ($n=19$; total response 20) answered that they strongly agreed, when asked if volunteering for the program had been a positive learning experience. In this survey, peer mentors were also asked if volunteering had been beneficial for their college experience; 70 percent ($n=14$) stated that they strongly agreed, and 30 percent ($n=6$) responded that they agreed. Lastly, 85 percent ($n=17$) stated that they were satisfied with the overall experience of volunteering with BAP. These results show that peer mentors find their experience working with BAP students to be both positive and beneficial.

Vocational services

According to *Autism Speaks*, nearly 90 percent of young adults with autism are unemployed, while an estimated 50,000 with autism disorders enter the workforce each year (Friedman 2014).

Vanbergeijk *et al.* (2008) state that a primary role of colleges and universities is to prepare students for employment. For students with ASD, this process should be a planned effort. The normal approach of doing formal interviews does not often work for individuals with ASD (Grandin 2012). Many students on the spectrum, whether in high school or college, have not had any opportunity to explore work or volunteer opportunities, or to build résumés (Wolf, Thierfeld Brown, and Bork 2009).

To address these issues, BAP students are offered a variety of vocational services including: vocational testing, individual and group vocational coaching, help obtaining on-campus jobs, and post-graduation referrals to agencies that specialize in vocational training and job placements for individuals with ASD.

BAP students are offered the opportunity to take a vocational testing battery that includes standardized interest, aptitude, personality, and executive functioning tests. These have been helpful in identifying possible careers and associated majors for students, as well as academic and vocational challenges that the student may face. Test results often confirm the path that the student is on, just as testing results have often pointed students in other directions.

Another important vocational service available to BAP students is a weekly "vocational group." At these meetings, students are offered help with résumé writing, job interview skills, or job-related concerns. Videotaped "mock interviews" have also been used to review and improve student presentations. Students are also encouraged to discuss their experiences in the workplace, whether positive or negative. All situations are reviewed in order to help students understand what is happening, and possible strategies for dealing with any problems or confusion they may report.

Gaining work experience in a controlled setting is important for individuals with ASD. Therefore, BAP partners with many offices and programs on the Adelphi campus, including the recreation center, the performing arts center, the library, and the office of information technology. These placements serve not only to give work experiences; they are indirect opportunities for the students to become part of the campus environment, social life, and culture.

As BAP has helped students move successfully towards graduation, the issue of post-graduation planning has become important. Individuals with ASD often struggle with the social components of the interview process, anxiety, or executive functioning issues that are judged during the process. To address these issues, and to help students move towards independence,

BAP has partnered with several private off-campus agencies that provide specifically designed vocational support services for individuals with ASD. In these programs, students receive vocational training and supervision, including job placement and job coaching support. The early results of these partnerships are promising. However, as with other transitions for individuals with ASD, the move from college to the workplace can be difficult. The challenges of accommodating for new people and new routines can cause anxiety (Harpur, Lawlor, and Fitzgerald 2004). This process can therefore often be daunting for both the students and the agencies involved.

Program challenges

As there are now more students identified with ASD, many of whom are qualified and who wish to attend post-secondary school, developing programs that are specifically designed to offer support for them has become increasingly important (Vanbergeijk et al. 2008). However, there are many obstacles and challenges to overcome in this process, both in designing the program, and in providing the best possible services for each student.

The first goal for any newly designed program for college students with ASD is to gain the support of the upper levels of administration, which must then set the tone for a welcoming and accepting campus culture (Nagler 2012). Administrators must understand and accept the fiscal and physical challenges and commitments needed to build a successful ASD program. Program directors must have the freedom to build an infrastructure of staff who are qualified and trained to provide services to this unique population. Ample space must also be available on campus to offer services, and to allow the program to grow.

As with other specialized support programs, administration must decide on the academic, social, and psychiatric criteria for the program, such as:

- » Will students have to meet the same academic criteria as other students to be accepted to the university?

- » Will there be a separate program application process that includes academic and psychiatric evaluations?

- » Will there be a separate fee for program services? If so, how will the fee be determined?

- » Once accepted, will students continue to have to meet the same academic demands as other students?

- » Will special classes be offered to program members, or will faculty staff be asked to modify classwork, assignments, or exams?

Programmatic questions also include the role, if any, that program staff will have interfacing with faculty and staff. Over the years, BAP students have often needed help with communications with faculty and university staff for in-class problems, which may have been based on poor understanding of social cues, poor impulse control, or anxieties, as well as executive functioning problems that have impacted on assignment completion or test performance.

Other areas for interaction with faculty and staff have been with:

- » on-campus living arrangements and/or roommate questions or problems

- » interpersonal and peer relationships

- » campus activities

- » financial services

- » academic accommodations

- » mental health counseling

- » career development.

On an individual basis, staff have had to develop wide and varied problem-solving approaches to dealing with the individual differences, academic and social, that this population presents with. Some consistent areas of difficulty have included student lack of reliability in attending their BAP meetings due to executive functioning dysfunction, and the persistent and pervasive dysfunctional thinking styles of many BAP students that have negatively impacted on their lives, including their academic and social behaviors and choices.

Past experiences and strategies that have been successful include the following:

» The use of CBT techniques and language has been helpful with students:

  › identifying the differences between problems and disasters

  › identifying and challenging cognitive distortions

  › encouraging students to "stay in the present" and avoiding thoughts of the past, and/or fears of the future

  › encouraging students to change thinking styles

  › encouraging students to engage in collaborative problem-solving techniques with staff.

» Unconditional positive regard, and acceptance by staff of student differences and challenges, has promoted strong alliances and trust with BAP students.

» Focusing on student strengths, rather than weaknesses, and encouraging creative thinking processes and activities has improved student self-esteem, and as a result, performance.

» Obtaining signed consent from students for BAP staff to communicate with faculty staff has been extremely helpful, both in problem-solving for students, and in helping faculty staff understand ASD students and develop helpful strategies.

» The use of graduate staff has minimized negative "transference" issues. Because the staff are close in age to the students, it is less likely that BAP students will identify the staff as authority or parental figures, and defensively respond to them as they would to their parents.

» Extended office hours have encouraged BAP students to feel that they have a safe haven on campus, and a place where they "belong."

» Regularly scheduled group parent meetings (that inform parents of program activities and services, and that address their anxieties about reduced access to faculty and staff and student information) have been helpful in creating successful partnerships with parents.

» Regular campus awareness and training sessions offered to university staff and faculty staff has led to greater acceptance and appreciation of BAP students.

CASE STUDY: BOB

The office of disability support services referred Bob to BAP as a second semester freshman. A math and physics major, Bob was on academic probation. Despite a successful high school career, and excellent standardized test scores, since arriving at Adelphi Bob had difficulty organizing and maintaining his work, and had become increasingly isolated. Prior to his referral to BAP, Bob had only used the office of disability support services for testing accommodations.

At his intake interview, Bob, who was living on campus, freely disclosed his diagnosis of ASD, and his feelings of frustration that after his successful high school career, he could not keep up with the demands of college.

During that meeting, Bob made poor eye contact, presented as unkempt, unshaven, and was wearing dirty and stained clothing. He reported that recently he had not been taking his medication reliably, and that he had only been eating "health bars" and drinking bottled water from vending machines for the past seven days. His classes included only math and physics classes, many of which started at 9am. Not surprisingly, his attendance was poor.

Bob kept a sketchpad on his lap during his meeting and often looked down and worked on a drawing: in this way he had filled many sketchpads. In fact, he preferred sketching to doing his schoolwork.

A schedule of BAP academic coaching and learning strategist meetings was created with Bob. He soon began to receive detailed, printed, schoolwork schedules, and assistance with assignment completion. Also, in his BAP meetings, Bob was assisted in making appointments to receive his academic accommodations, such as extra test-taking time and a distraction-reduced testing environment, which he had not been accessing.

Bob's personal care and dietary habits improved when alarms were set on his cell phone to remind him to take his medication. His academic coach also encouraged him to get a small refrigerator for his dorm room, so that he could get food from the cafeteria and campus convenience store during off hours, so that he did not have to deal with the crowds and noise that had been causing him sensory overload.

Bob began meeting with a peer mentor, and became involved in campus activities and clubs. He attended the BAP social group meetings regularly, developed friendships with several other BAP students, and became roommates with two of them.

Bob was also scheduled for vocational testing. The results of his tests indicated low aptitudes for, and little interest in, the engineering career path that his parents had put him on. Instead, he showed clear preferences for, and high skills in, science and art-related fields.

After a meeting with Bob and his parents to review his progress in BAP, and the results of his vocational testing,

Bob changed his major to art. His career path was defined by his interest in working in a career in video games, hopefully designing game characters.

As Bob's career at Adelphi continued, though he continued to struggle with executive functioning issues such as getting to classes and turning his work in on time, his academic performance and reliability steadily rose, as did his grades. Bob not only graduated with a GPA (grade point average) of 3.0, he also received his Master's in art, and is now pursuing a career as a graphic animator.

CASE STUDY: SAM

Sam enrolled in BAP as a freshman on acceptance to Adelphi. In his intake interview, he presented as clean and well-groomed, able to express himself well, with a clear and defined interest in pursuing a career in accounting. While Sam made excellent eye contact, he reported anxiety about the transition from high school to college, and his ability to be successful in college. Sam's greatest ongoing challenge was continuing and debilitating fears of failure, and of the future. His negative thoughts overcame him regularly, often to the point of executive functioning dysfunction, and failure to produce or turn in assignments.

Sam, who lived at home and commuted to school, also struggled with perseverative worries of disappointing his family, and not living up to what he believed to be their expectations for him. Because he struggled with understanding social relationships and social cues, he often misunderstood what his family was trying to communicate, and incorrectly believed that he had disappointed them, which caused him to feel increased anxiety and depression.

Sam responded well to CBT strategies such as cognitive restructuring, perspective-taking and self-monitoring skills, and limited requests for him to act against his anxieties.

Sam's experience in BAP was marked by his consistent willingness to try staff suggestions. He reliably attended his BAP academic coaching and learning strategy meetings. He responded well to the collaborative approach his academic coach used to create clear and concrete weekly schoolwork schedules. Also, though not all worked for him, Sam was willing to try all the strategies that his learning strategist suggested. Sam also regularly attended BAP group meetings and activities, and met regularly with his peer mentor. Sam has graduated with a degree in business administration and is now pursuing a Master's degree.

Research

Research regarding college students with ASD is substantially lacking in publications to date; various literature reviews on the subject have voiced exhortations for further research considering the burgeoning number of students on the spectrum who are now, or soon to be, enrolled in college (Glennon 2001; Trembath *et al.* 2012; Vanbergeijk *et al.* 2008). Research by BAP responds to these issues by conducting focused empirical studies centering on the students enrolled in BAP who self-disclose with ASD / non-verbal learning disorders. Empirical study, data collection, and analysis are essential to the evaluation and development of BAP.

The Bridges research team strives to coordinate original and innovating projects in the pursuit of elucidating the academic, social, emotional, and vocational experiences of their students on the spectrum; in doing so they aspire to develop a more comprehensive understanding of their strengths, weaknesses, challenges, and successes. They also aim to contribute to public awareness of the experiences relating to college students identifying with ASD by disseminating their research throughout the fields of psychology and education, through publications and at conferences.

The two major areas of interest in terms of broad research perspectives concern the efficacy of BAP and its usefulness for students, as well as the personal experiences of the students in multifarious respects. Another area of interest concerns the students' vocational/independent advances post-graduation from Adelphi.

BAP was first established in 2007, and so, as of 2014, students are now beginning to graduate. Collecting data concerning their post-graduation pursuits (whether this includes vocational placements/interests, higher education, or otherwise) is salient information regarding the advancement of the program. Along with guiding the students to succeed academically, as a program Bridges is also dedicated to encouraging students to develop independent aspirations post-graduation that will be a good fit for them individually. Research on student involvement post-graduation will increase in the years to come as more students graduate.

Current research

Presently Bridges reseach is focused on a longitudinal assessment of the program. The longitudinal assessment of BAP is now summarized, and some statistics discussed as an overview.

BAP OUTCOME STUDY

This five-year longitudinal assessment is tracking a cohort of Bridges students who first enrolled in the program for the Fall 2012 semester ($n=17$). The purpose of this research is to evaluate the efficacy of the program by analyzing the progress of this group in three major respects: GPA, attendance percentage, and Rosenberg Self-esteem Score (RSES; Rosenberg 1965). The program population as a whole is also documented and compared ($n=75$). Individual semesters are paired in analyses to determine variable changes/consistencies as the students move forward through Adelphi and, in turn, BAP. This data is also utilized to determine retention percentage and total meetings offered each year, among other related statistics. Some available statistics that have been determined as data collection continues are discussed briefly below.

As of the end of the Fall 2013 semester, 2917 mandatory meetings were held during the 15 weeks of the semester. This included 1352 individual academic coaching sessions (IACSs) and 1565 individual learning strategy sessions (ILSSs). There were a total of 6453 mandatory sessions within the year as a whole with the Fall 2012, Spring 2013, and Fall 2013 semesters combined, which includes all IACSs and ILSSs.

Currently, the Fall 2012 cohort was tracked for three complete semesters (Fall 2012, Spring 2013, and Fall 2013). The data reveals significant positive changes for RSES and IACS attendance. Over the course of three semesters, the percentage of IACSs increased, with the average attendance for all three at 80.81 percent. The average percentage for the Fall 2012 semester is 84.93 percent, the Spring 2013 semester average is 67.80 percent, and the Fall 2013 semester average is 89.71 percent ($f=3.721; p=<0.05$), where a total of 15 students were included in the analysis.

In addition to attendance percentage, students are also assessed for their level of self-esteem, which is measured using the RSES, and is distributed to every student in the program at the beginning of each semester. The Fall 2012 cohort was specifically tracked for changes in their score across semesters. A score of 15 and above represents healthy self-esteem. Scores for all three semesters are listed as follows: the average score for the Fall 2012 semester is 14.50, the Spring 2013 semester average is 13.30, and the Fall 2013 semester average is 19.90 ($f=10.725; p=<0.01$). This states that students are evaluating themselves more positively after one year in the program than they did in earlier semesters.

GPA and ILSS attendance remained consistent for the Fall 2012 cohort; they maintained an average GPA of 3.29 ($n=15$) for three semesters, and attended 79.0 percent ($n=14$) of learning strategy sessions.

ADDITIONAL DATA COLLECTION

Data collection has also determined that as of the Fall 2013 semester, retention was at 89 percent for the population as a whole. First semester retention was at 92 percent, and one-year retention was documented at 82.36 percent. The retention rate for the university as a whole was 94.5 percent for the first semester, and 81.1 percent for the first year.

Personal statements and accounts of students' opinions and experiences of BAP are pivotal in our efficacy research—student satisfaction is crucial for the success of the program. To evaluate satisfaction, a student satisfaction survey was designed and solicited.

A total of 60.0 percent of students who participated in the survey ($n= 21$, when total responses $= 36$) stated that they were very satisfied with the services they received through Bridges, and 34.3 percent ($n=12$) that they were satisfied; 47.2 percent ($n=17$) indicated that they strongly agreed that BAP had made a positive difference in the quality of their life. When asked if BAP had helped them to appreciate and develop their strengths as a college student, 42.9 percent ($n=15$) strongly agreed.

When asked if they could think of any other services that they would like Bridges to offer, many expressed that more intensive social skills training would be an excellent addition—they thought that this would help students to progress socially. Students also expressed how important Bridges social events were to them, and suggested adding more of these events to the schedule.

Future for Bridges research

In the future, Bridges research is looking to advance the program as a whole by applying empirical findings to clinical practice, and sharing these findings with the psychological and educational research communities. As more data is collected from upcoming studies, they will be able to develop their understanding concerning the students' experiences and the impact BAP has had on their lives in various respects, during and after college. While more students graduate, their information on their graduation rates and post-graduation pursuits will become more meaningful, and they will gain further insight into helping their students in achieving their goals.

Summary

As awareness and screening techniques improve, early identification increases, and students receive more services from kindergarten to twelfth grade, the population of qualified college students with ASD increases. Therefore, the need for defined support programs for college students with ASD will continue to grow. These programs must not only have full administrative support on campus, but they must also take a comprehensive approach to services provided, and be flexible enough to meet the unique needs of this population. Gaining administrative support for developing professional staff, and the growing need for space, will likely be a challenge to begin and respond to program growth on most campuses. However, as early research results and positive outcomes suggest, such programs can be successful.

References

Adreon, D. and Durocher, J.S. (2007) "Evaluating the college transition needs of individuals with high-functioning autism spectrum disorders." *Intervention in School and Clinics 42*(271).

APA (American Psychiatric Association) (2013) *The Diagnostic and Statistical Manual of Mental Disorders* (5th edn) (DSM-5). Arlington, VA: American Psychiatric Publishing.

Bandura, A. (1977) *Social Learning Theory*. Englewood Cliffs, NJ: Prentice-Hall.

Beck, A., Rush, A., Shaw, B., and Emery, G. (1979) *Cognitive Theory of Depression*. New York: Guilford Press.

Blumberg, S., Bramlett, M., Kogan, M., Maternal and Child Health Bureau, *et al.* (2013) "Changes in prevalence of parent-reported autism spectrum disorder in school-aged US children: 2007 to 2011–2012." *National Health Statistics Reports 65.*

Friedman, D. (2014) "How my son's autism inspired business innovation." Monday, January 1. *Autism Speaks.* Available at www.autismspeaks.org/blog/2014/01/13/how-my-sons-autism-inspired-business-innovation

Glennon, T.J. (2001) "Stress of the university experience for students with Asperger syndrome." *Work: A Journal of Prevention, Assessment and Rehabilitation 17, 3*, 183–190.

Grandin, T. (2012) *Different...Not Less.* Arlington, TX: Future Horizons Inc.

Harpur, J., Lawlor, M., and Fitzgerald, M. (2004) *Succeeding in College with Asperger Syndrome.* London: Jessica Kingsley Publishers.

Nagler, M. (2012) "Blueprint for an Asperger syndrome college support program." *Autism Spectrum News 4, 4.*

Nagler, M. and Shore, S. (2013) "Supporting students on the autism spectrum in higher education." *Autism Spectrum News 5*, 3.

Rogers, C.R. (1961) *On Becoming a Person*. Boston, MA: Houghton Mifflin.

Rosenberg, M. (1965) *Society and the Adolescent Self-image*. Princeton, NJ: Princeton University Press.

Trembath, D., Germano, C., Johanson, G., and Dissanayake, C. (2012) "The experience of anxiety in young adults with autism spectrum disorders." *Hammill Institute on Disabilities 27*, 4, 213–224.

Vanbergeijk, E., Klin, A., and Volkmar, F. (2008) "Supporting more able students on the autism spectrum: College and beyond." *Journal of Autism and Developmental Disorders 38*, 1359–1370.

Welkowitz, L.A. and Bakes, L.J. (2005) "Supporting college students with Asperger's Syndrome." In L.J. Baker and L.A Welkowitz (eds) *Asperger's Syndrome: Intervening in Schools, Clinics, and Communities* (pp.173–187). Mahwah, NJ: Erlbaum.

Wolf, L., Thierfeld Brown, J., and Bork, G. (2009) *Students with Asperger Syndrome: A Guide for College Personnel*. Lenexa, KS: Autism Asperger Publishing Co.

VOICES FROM THE FIELD

Experiences of Students Written in Their Own Words

9

Struggling with Disability and Dealing with Family

Melissa Mooney

My childhood

My name is Melissa, and I have been living with multiple disabilities for most of my life. I am on the autism spectrum, I've overcome post-traumatic stress disorder (PTSD), survived a debilitating case of Lyme disease, and I am also diagnosed with pseudotumor cerebri, attention deficit hyperactivity disorder (ADHD), and epilepsy. My life has been a struggle since the day I was conceived. My parents met at an Alcoholics Anonymous meeting. They suffered with mental illness, and battled their demons throughout my childhood. I spent many nights awake listening to their fighting, which often broke out into violence. I lost count of how many times the police were called to our home. My parents would scream and yell, curse, threaten, wrestle each other, and break things. Sometimes my siblings and I couldn't come out of our rooms in the morning because there would be broken glass all over the floor. A few times my father was arrested, even though my mother was just as violent as he was. Sometimes, when a fight wasn't going her way, she would barricade herself in the bathroom, and threaten to kill herself. I remember being as young as four when I saw my mother overdose for the first time. One night, during a really bad fight, I heard my dad break down the bathroom door, and he rushed my mother out of the house. When I heard them drive away I came out of my bedroom to find blood all over the floor from my mother cutting herself. She was hospitalized at an in-patient psychiatric unit off and on throughout my childhood, and sometimes I would visit her there. She and I were never close. She was a very needy individual, and as a baby I couldn't show her the love that she desired. Children with autism have difficulty with reciprocal social interaction, and just like many children on the autism spectrum, I didn't display a lot of affection. That really upset her. I've been told by relatives that when I was at a very young age my mother stopped caring for me, and my older sister became my caregiver. My mother wanted nothing to do with me. She didn't love me, cuddle me, or praise me when I did something right. She resented me for not being "normal." I was an odd child, and she didn't want a freak for a kid. She regularly reminded me of that, saying I was retarded, cursing me, calling me names, and putting me down. My older sister and younger brother were both fairly "normal." My brother was a child genius, and my parents adored him. They didn't understand why I couldn't be more like him. He was the smartest kid in school, and I was a failure.

My schooling

Even in kindergarten I knew that I was different. I didn't act like the other kids, and I couldn't relate to them on any level. My behavior was rambunctious, and I couldn't hold a conversation without saying things that were bizarre. I was easily overstimulated, and would engage in self-stimulating behaviors (stimming), such as rocking and screaming. Whenever I played games with the other kids I would ruin the game by playing according to my own rules, and not participating in teamwork. My teachers would get angry at me for that, and I would be removed from participating with the other kids. My classmates called me obnoxious, "motor mouth," and "looney-gooney." In first grade I finally made a friend, but she would only be my friend if I kept it a secret. Our agreement was that she could be mean to me and make fun of me with the other kids: but we could only be friends when nobody else was around to witness our friendship. I was so desperate for friendship that I gladly went along with it. We were neighbors, and after school, when other kids weren't around, she would invite me over to play at her house. I loved her house, because she had all sorts of toys, games, and girly things that I didn't have at my house. She collected plush kittens that I fell in love with, because I've always been obsessed with cats. She let me play with all of her stuff, and didn't criticize me when I acted weird. I later found out that her sister was also on the autism spectrum, so maybe that's why she was nice to me when we played together. Aside from when we were at school, she was the only girl my age who treated me like a friend. I made other friends, but they were usually much younger than me. By the time I was in fifth grade my closest friends were five and six years old. Even though the neighbors would never let their children over to my house, they still let me come over to play at theirs. We would climb trees, color on the sidewalk with chalk, and play Nintendo together. I loved playing with them, and hated whenever I had to go home. At home I spent a lot of time playing by myself in the attic. My parents had turned it into my own personal playroom where I could be alone. That way I couldn't annoy anybody. In the attic my stuffed animals were my best friends, and we would draw and color for hours.

As bad as elementary school was, middle school was a whole new ball game. Kids went from being mean to being bullies. My "secret friend" from elementary school no longer wanted to be my friend at all. The more she picked on me in front of the other girls, the more they liked her. It became entertainment for them to see me upset, and they wouldn't stop picking on me until I was visibly angry or sad. I walked funny, so they would imitate my walk whenever they saw me in the hallway. They would make fun of the way I dressed, because I wasn't into trends, and I didn't wear make-up. They laughed at me for not knowing how to do my hair. What sixth grader doesn't know how to braid? In class they would wait until the teacher wasn't looking, and push all of my books off the desk. The bullying was so bad that even my parents were concerned. They took me out of public school, and put me into private school.

The kids in private school were a lot more disciplined and composed than the kids in public school. Even in private school I never paid attention to the lesson. I was in my own little world, daydreaming, doodling, and being a distraction to my peers. I couldn't concentrate during tests, and failed a lot of them. My teachers complained to my parents, and urged them to have me evaluated for ADHD. A doctor diagnosed me, and put me on Ritalin. I don't remember the Ritalin having any effect on me, and my performance didn't improve. One day I was talking to a boy, and I commented that he had a square head. I didn't mean it as an insult; it was literally square in proportion. However, the school administrators wouldn't tolerate such a comment, and they kicked me out of school. At that point my parents had no choice but to home school me. I loved being home schooled, because I didn't have to put up with bullies anymore. The only bullies left were my family members, but I was used to that. I could spend as much time alone as I wanted, and I could be myself without having to worry about getting into trouble with teachers. Both of my parents worked, so home school consisted of me administering Hooked on Phonics® and Hooked on Math® to myself. I was good at language and arts, but I was bad at math. I was in sixth grade, and didn't even know basic addition. However, my math skills sky-rocketed with Hooked on Math®, because it was rote memorization, and I was good at rote memorization. All day I would sit with my stuffed animals repeating flash cards over and over again. I didn't miss regular school at all.

Family and emotional struggles

At the end of sixth grade my parents decided to get a divorce. I was devastated. Even though I hated their fighting, I didn't want things to change. My brother and I moved with my mother into a small apartment two towns away. I fell into a deep depression. I stopped doing my schoolwork, and developed a negative attitude. Separating from my father, moving, and becoming a single mom threw my mother into a bad mental state. She became even more hostile, violent, and negligent towards me. She didn't have my father to beat up on anymore, and with all of my deficiencies, I was an easy target. She saw my depression as defiance, and punished me for it. She told me not to come into her eyesight, because she didn't want to see my sad, ugly face. She figured that my lack of academic motivation was due to me spending my time playing around. So she threw away my belongings. I slacked on my chores, so she dumped bags of garbage on me, saying that if I wanted to live like a dog, she would treat me like a dog. Who dumps garbage on their dog? If she had a hard day at work, I was the first person she came to when she got home. She would scream obscenities at me, degrade me, and threaten me with violence. She told me that she wanted to kill me, because life in prison would be better than having a child like me. For reasons unknown, she put me back in school. I was glad because with everything going on, I would do anything to get away from home.

I started eighth grade determined to make a good impression so that I wouldn't have the same experiences I had had in sixth grade. I studied the other girls, and tried to adopt their ways. If they said a phrase that made other kids laugh, I would take note so that I could use that phrase in my own interactions with kids. Unfortunately, I would use the phrases at the wrong times, and instead of laughing, people would just look at me funny. I tried harder to pay attention to trends, but never managed to pull it off. For example, tube tops were popular when I was in eighth grade. I didn't have any tube tops, so I wore a skirt as a shirt. In my mind that was close enough, but to everyone else, it was ridiculous. Pretty soon people were being mean to me again, but I didn't complain, because I would rather be at school being bullied than trapped in my apartment. Teachers became aware of the bullying, and instead of intervening, they referred me to the guidance counselor's office. During one of our conversations, the topic of my home life came up, and I spoke about my mother's behavior. I didn't know that the guidance counselor would call child protective services.

A social worker came to our apartment, and interviewed my mother. My mother was a good con artist, and sweet-talked the social worker into believing that I was lying to get attention since I had just lost my father to divorce. That was the end of the investigation. After that, my mother's rage exploded. How dare I have child protective services called on her! If I wanted to tell people that I was being abused and neglected, she was going to show me what true abuse and neglect was. My belongings were once again thrown away. She made me sleep on the kitchen floor without a blanket. I wasn't allowed to eat regular meals. I was put on a diet where most meals consisted of a grapefruit, and occasionally I would get a side of spinach. She refused to call me by my real name, and referred to me as "bitch" instead. All house chores became my responsibility, and if they weren't done perfectly, repercussions were severe. I started to develop severe panic attacks and anger outbursts at school. I spent a lot of time in the school nurse's office, because I became easily overwhelmed and anxious. I didn't pay attention in class anyway, so I wasn't missing much. I no longer cared about winning friendships, so when kids bullied me, I lashed out at them. My behavior got so bad that I was eventually expelled from school. My emotional disturbance fed into my mother's emotional disturbance, and the more trouble I got into, the worse she abused me. One night, when she was fighting with me, the police were called, and they walked in on my mother beating me. Child protective services finally took me away.

Child protective services tried to implement a plan that would improve my home situation and relationship with my mother so that I could return home, but eventually my mother gave up. She couldn't care for a child with a developmental disability suffering from emotional disturbance, and she surrendered guardianship to the state. There aren't a lot of foster parents willing to adopt children with special needs, so I was placed into a therapeutic group home where specialists could help me with my challenges.

At first I had a difficult time adjusting to being in the foster care system, and I got moved around a lot, because I wouldn't cooperate with any of the programs. I was placed in a residential treatment center for kids with emotional disturbances. The method of care there was "tough love," which was later deemed abusive, and the center was shut down. While I was there I was subjected to over-medication, take-downs and restraints that left me with injuries and long periods of seclusion. None of those techniques helped me to manage my symptoms or behavior.

The medication zombified me to the point where I couldn't process or learn anything. Take-downs and restraints triggered severe sensory overload, which only made my outbursts worse. Sometimes seclusion helped, because it was a low-stimulus environment that allowed me to decompress. However, being left there for hours and hours was pointless when I only needed a few minutes to calm down. Luckily, I was taken out of the center, and placed back into a therapeutic group home. Even though I had difficulty adjusting to new environments, over time I realized that I was being given an opportunity to become a better person and to live a better life. I was placed on low-dose medication that helped curb my anxiety and depression, and therapists helped me develop coping strategies for managing my symptoms. I learned that a lot of my outbursts were due to my inability to express myself effectively. Since I had trouble verbally communicating, they taught me that I could write what I was feeling. If I was angry about something, I could write about it instead of acting it out. They helped me identify sensory and emotional triggers, and taught me to remove myself from overwhelming situations. I went back to school, and for the first time I was given an Individualized Education Program (IEP).

High school

I had never heard of an IEP before, and I had never been given accommodations at school in the past. The most effective accommodation they had given me was permission to exit the classroom to work in a resource room. The resource room was a quiet room where I could work one-on-one with a special education teacher. There were never a lot of students in the resource room, so I felt more at ease about doing my schoolwork there. If students in the regular classroom were being mean to me, I could go to the resource room instead of having to put up with them. If the classroom environment was too overwhelming, I could go to the resource room to decompress. If a particular assignment or test was giving me a panic attack, I could go to the resource room and get help. It was my escape from bullies, classroom distractions, and test anxiety. With this accommodation in place I had a much easier time getting through assignments and functioning in the school setting. My grades excelled, and in one year I went from being a special education student to being an honors student. In all my life I never expected that I could ever be in honors classes, but once I got the help that I needed, that's exactly where I wound up. I realized that, even though I had been raised to believe I was stupid and incapable of doing anything productive with my life, I was intelligent, and perfectly capable of doing anything I put my mind to. For the first time, I had a sense of self-importance, and it felt good. I wondered if there were any limitations to what I could do, and when other students began to talk about college, I thought maybe there was a chance that I could go to college, too. I didn't want to go to college for the sake of getting a degree; I wanted to go for the sake of proving to everyone who thought I was incapable of being successful wrong. When I told my social worker that I wanted to apply to college, she laughed, and told me that it was unrealistic to think that someone like me could do well in college. I knew she was wrong, and I planned on applying anyway. My mind was made up.

Another accommodation that I received from my IEP was participation in a special social group just for students who shared similar challenges to the ones that I struggled with. I found that it was much easier to relate to those kids than the "normal" kids, and I made a few friends. One of them became my best friend, and we spent a lot of time together. His family was kind to me, and they would take me out to the movies, to visit museums, and to play putt-putt golf (crazy golf). Eventually they decided that they would like to informally adopt me, and they invited me to live with them. They took care of my needs, and they were supportive of my desire to go to college. I didn't know anything about applying to college, but they were very encouraging, and vowed to help me with the process. My friend's mom was a high school music teacher, but she also played piano for local college theatrical productions. Even though I didn't know about the local colleges, she did, and she told me all about them. She even offered to put a good word in for me. She helped me fill out requests for information from three colleges that she felt were suited to give me the help that I needed.

One of the colleges had a tiger as the mascot, and I was instantly sold. Their mascot was a cat, and I loved cats. I didn't care about anything else, that was my top choice. I still went through the application process for all three of them, though. My friend's mom sat with me filling out the forms, and helping me formulate my goals statements. Once I was finished with my goals statements, she combined them with all of the other necessary documentation, and mailed them to the colleges for me. I was anxious to find out if any of them would accept me, and I waited for what seemed like an eternity to get a response. The first letter I received was from my top choice, the college with the tiger mascot. Sadly, it was a rejection letter. I was somewhat devastated, but at the same time hopeful that one of the other two colleges would still accept me. The second letter came, and it was also a rejection letter. At that point I started to panic. Two out of three colleges had already rejected me. The third college was a private college. If I couldn't get into the public college, how was I going to get into a private one? My friend's mom was very active at that college, and before I could receive a third rejection letter, she went to the college to advocate for me. She talked to them about my history, and explained the discrepancies in my records. She told them how my past performance was not a fair indicator of my true abilities, and how I had flourished into a dedicated honors student in the past year. We waited another few weeks to receive their response, and when it finally arrived, it was an acceptance letter. I was overjoyed!

College

Despite being overjoyed, I was also scared. It was a major transition, and I would be living on my own for the first time. My social worker and therapist helped me to prepare for the transition. My therapist contacted the college to request that I have a private dorm. My social challenges would make it difficult to live with a roommate, and I needed a retreat where I could be by myself, to decompress from any stress that I would face. My social worker took me shopping for school supplies and things I would need for my dorm. Since I had never lived on my own, I wasn't sure what I would need, so it was nice to have someone who had experienced college dorm living to help me prepare. She taught me that the more organized my belongings were, the easier it would be to manage independent living and schoolwork. She picked out small plastic shelving units that would be labeled according to the contents inside. She also got different colored pens and highlighters so that I would have an easier time keeping track of the most important information. She let me choose notebooks and folders that had cats on them, which would help me stay calm if I was stressed out in class. I also picked out bedding and linen that were my favorite colors so that I could make my dorm my own. The more familiar we made my dorm, the easier it would be to settle there. Finally, my social worker gathered all of the food and cleaning supplies I would need. She told me that I would need to utilize the library and computer labs to complete my work. This made me anxious, because I knew the library and computer labs would be full of other students. To my surprise, my social worker found an old computer that wasn't being used, and gave it to me so that I could do my schoolwork in private. I was as ready as I would ever be.

Even though I had all of the supplies I would need, nothing could prepare me for the chaos of moving day. Hundreds of students with their families were carrying their belongings from their vehicles to their dorms. The dorm building was full of people hustling to move in and prepare their space. There were loud conversations, and people yelling back and forth down the halls. Orientation leaders kept trying to talk to me, introducing themselves, and asking me questions that I wasn't prepared to answer. It was all so overwhelming that I had to shut myself in my dorm room, and wait for things to calm down outside. Once I had all of my stuff moved in, I spent the rest of the evening alone to process the events of the day. Other girls were out in the hallway introducing themselves to each other, and chattering about all sorts of meaningless things, but I needed time to let everything sink in. I was officially a college student. Wow! The following day was the new student orientation. I sat in the back of the auditorium to avoid having to talk to strangers, and when we went on the campus tour, I trailed behind the group so that I wouldn't get stuck in the middle of the crowd. After the orientation was a meet-and-greet dinner where new students could talk to professors. I found an empty table away from the professors and other students where I could eat in peace. Much to my disappointment I was ushered over to a table where a biology professor was talking to a few students. I remained composed on the outside as I panicked on the inside. The students at the table spoke so eloquently, and they seemed so confident. When the conversation turned to me I tried to mimic their confidence, inventing aspirations on the spot, and dropping every big word I knew. I must not have been very convincing, because they looked at me funny, and then carried on the conversation amongst themselves, as if I wasn't there. It was the first day, and I had already made a bad impression. One day I was called into the assistant dean's office, and she reprimanded me for my attire. The other students dressed nicely, while I dressed for comfort. I liked to wear sweat pants with a t-shirt, but she wanted me to wear dresses and khakis. I asked her if she was going to buy them for me, and that ended the conversation.

I couldn't wait for classes to start, because for all that I lacked in social skills I made up for in academic ability. I took a variety of courses, from philosophy to dance. I wasn't very coordinated, so maybe dance wasn't the best choice, but the professor was really helpful and understanding. However, my chemistry teacher was not. Chemistry class involved daily group work, and I didn't know how to function in a group. I sat quietly listening to my group members shoot ideas back and forth with each other so fast that I couldn't keep up. By the time I could process the first concept of the lesson, they were already ten steps ahead. When I was given an exam, I just stared at the paper, unable to comprehend anything that was on it. It didn't help that the tests were timed, because the clock ticking down gave me so much anxiety I couldn't focus even if I wanted to. By the time midterms came around I was already failing. I spoke to my therapist about it, and she contacted my advisor to discuss having accommodations put into place.

It was a private college, so they weren't bound by the same disability requirements as public colleges. However, they agreed to supplement group work with one-on-one time with the professor, and they gave me extended time on tests. Unfortunately, the accommodations came too late to redeem my chemistry grade, and I received an "F" for that class. I was crushed. It was my first semester of college, and I failed. Not to mention I still hadn't made any friends. My dream of being a successful college student was crumbling, and I became severely depressed. The depression and stress put me into a bad mental state, and I started to have flashbacks and nightmares from my past. I would lie in bed crying, fighting anxiety that was so bad it felt like a rabid animal was clawing me from the inside out. Nightmares kept me from sleeping, and I spent my days exhausted. I often had to leave my child psychology class, because the subjects of parenting and child abuse would put me into a flashback. I would hide in the bathroom reliving my trauma. PTSD consumed me to the point where I couldn't function. I wasn't eating, I wasn't sleeping, and I wasn't doing my schoolwork. The daily torment of PTSD made me suicidal, and during summer break I was sent to a specialized trauma disorders inpatient psychiatric unit. Even though they didn't cure my PTSD, I came out of there better equipped to manage my symptoms. At the start of my second year of college I was ready to do a better job, and be the awesome student I knew I could be.

As determined as I was to improve in my second year, I started to become very sick physically. I started to have joint pain, muscle spasms, fatigue, and respiratory infections. Some mornings I couldn't get out of bed no matter how hard I tried, and on days that I went to class, the short walk between classes was so painful that I had to sit down many times along the way. I went to see a doctor, but he chalked it up as being a physical manifestation of my psychological stress. In other words, it was all in my head. As months passed I continued to get sicker and sicker. I felt like I was dying. I lost the ability to walk on my own, and had to use a walker which would eventually become a wheelchair. I took so much pain medicine that I developed ulcers. My respiratory infections would get so bad that I would be sent to the hospital to get nebulizer treatments to help me breathe. One day I was talking to a nurse, and she asked me if I had ever been tested for Lyme disease. I hadn't even heard of Lyme disease. I had recently found a new doctor, and I mentioned it to him. In the end, it turned out to be Lyme disease, and I was put on a variety of medications, including multiple antibiotics. Even though the disease had been identified, and I was receiving treatment, my poor academic performance would no longer be tolerated. There were so many reasons for them to dismiss me from the college that they finally did.

I had nowhere to go. I had aged out of the foster care system, and my friend's house was off limits, because they were facing bad circumstances themselves. So I wound up in a homeless shelter. This was my rock bottom. I had no family, my health was poor, and I had lost college. I moved from shelter to shelter, and every shelter had its own unique set of problems. Some housed violent drug addicts; some provided only shelter with no care. I was getting nowhere with my life. I couldn't stay like that. I had to go back to college. I decided to reapply. I obtained an application for my original first choice, the college with the tiger mascot. I remembered the steps to filling out and submitting the application, and was able to do it on my own. Once I sent in the application I prayed and prayed that I would get in. I had to get in. It was my last chance. After a few months I received a packet in the mail from the college. It was a packet, not a letter! I couldn't believe it. Even though they had originally rejected me, for some reason they decided to accept me this time. Like my first college, my tuition was paid through loans and grants. Unlike my first college, my new college gave financial aid refunds for any funds that exceeded the cost of tuition. My refunds were large enough to live off, and instead of living in the dorms, I decided that it would be better for me to live on my own. I found a small house in a poor part of town where I could rent a room for really cheap. I was being given a fresh start, and a new chance to be a successful college student.

I had learned enough from my experiences at my first college to know some ways to help myself. I immediately applied for disability accommodations. I received testing in a quiet environment, extended time on tests, permission to exit the classroom as needed, and mobility transportation. I spoke with my professors upfront about the challenges that I faced with my disabilities, and for the most part, they were understanding. I was advocating for myself, and that may have been the most important thing I learned in college. I worked harder than ever, and my grades reflected it. My good grades gave me a boost in confidence, and the more my confidence grew, the more I applied myself. When it came time for me to decide my major, I wasn't sure what I wanted to do. I thought about what my skills were, what I could apply prior knowledge and experience to, and what I thought would be a rewarding career.

I decided to major in special education, because I was a special education student myself. I knew the differences between methods of teaching that worked and those that didn't work, because I had first-hand experience. I was able to weigh in on topics with which I had personal experience, whereas the other students only had textbook knowledge. That made a huge difference. My unique experience put me ahead of the rest of the class. The work was easy to me, because it was already part of who I was. I did so well that I made it onto the Dean's List. Before I knew it, I was preparing for my student teaching internship. I was already at the top of my class, and I was sure I would do well. As sure as I was, my professors were not. They spoke to me about the differences between schoolwork and professional work. They tried to convey that becoming a teacher meant I had to learn professionalism. I didn't know what it meant to be a professional; I had only ever been a student. I had a meeting with my internship advisor, and she told me that I was going to have to work on eliminating the outward symptoms of my autism. That meant I had to be able to look people in the eye, and I had to stop rocking, because it was bad modeling for children who were also on the autism spectrum. I needed to learn how to remove all emotionality from how I handled conflict and stress. Finally, I had to learn how to function in a setting where I had no accommodations.

I started working with an occupational therapist to help me learn to make eye contact, and to manage sensory symptoms without stimming in ways that were as obvious as rocking. She taught me that I could still find relieving sensory input through stretching, and if I stretched at regular intervals throughout the day, I wouldn't have as much urge to rock. If I really needed to stim, I could go into the bathroom and do it privately. Despite all of my occupational therapist's efforts, I never learned how to make eye contact. It was just too painful, and I couldn't concentrate on what someone was saying if I was busy forcing myself to look them in the eye. When it came to shopping for a professional wardrobe, I didn't rely on my own sense of style (or lack thereof). When I went to the stores I asked the employees to help me, and they picked out some nice outfits.

On my first day of my internship I was assigned to a classroom of preschoolers with developmental disabilities. I was so excited! I would be working with my own kind. At first it was wonderful. I saw myself in a lot of the children, and was able to identify with them more than the other teachers could. If a child displayed a behavior that baffled them, I was able to recognize what the function of the behavior was, what symptoms the child was struggling with, and what intervention strategies would be most helpful. Despite my ability to help the children, though, the lead teacher didn't want to adopt my methods. She had her own way of doing things, but her way did more harm than good. If the child had difficulty paying attention, she would yell at them, or slap them on the head. If a child stood up in the middle of story time, she would kick them back down. If a child was stimming too much, or being hyperactive, she would put them in a restraint chair, and leave them there. If a child had sensory processing dysfunction, she would use a squirt bottle as a means of punishing them. The more time I spent in the classroom, the more horrified I became. It was so bad that I had no choice but to report the lead teacher's behavior. I thought I was doing the right thing by protecting the children, but little did I know that reporting child abuse in a school is like opening Pandora's box.

First, I was removed from my student teaching internship. My internship advisor told me that I was not allowed to discuss what had happened with anyone, especially not the parents of the children. However, when parents came to me concerned about their children, I couldn't lie to them or hide it. They deserved to know the truth, so I told them. The school board began an investigation. Not only were they investigating what had happened in the classroom, but they were also investigating me to find out if I had any credibility. Somehow, they were able to dig up my history in the foster care system, as well as my diagnoses. The school principal sent a letter to the parents, which was later shown to me. It told them about my past, and claimed that I was a very troubled person. It said that I was "mentally deficient" because I was on the autism spectrum. It said that my perception of the lead teacher's behavior as being abusive was the result of my inexperience in the field. He called me a liar, and erased any credibility I had. My loss of credibility, coupled with my defiance in speaking to the parents, lost me my student teaching internship. I was not allowed to continue on my path to becoming a special education teacher. I remember one of my classmates saying that it was better that way, because an autistic teacher trying to help autistic children was like the blind leading the blind. I wasn't being dismissed from the college, but I was equally as devastated. I had worked so hard, and come so far to achieve my dreams, only to have it all come to an abrupt end. How could I move on? How could I start over? What path would I take to achieve my goal of helping children with special needs?

Employment

I decided to change my major to psychology. I could become a child psychologist, and help children with special needs without being hassled by the corruption of the education system. It had taken me so long to get through the teaching program that I ran out of financial aid, so I had to get a job to pay my tuition fees. I was hired at a major retailer, where I organized shelves and worked as a cashier. I enjoyed organizing the shelves. It was a systematic and repetitive job where I got to make everything look nice. My favorite section was the cat food section. I spent hours turning every single can facing forward, all while being surrounded by images of cats. My co-workers made fun of me. They didn't understand my obsession, nor did they understand why I was so awkward. I was the butt of many jokes. I struggled the most when I worked on the cash register. I had to come into contact with hundreds of people a day, with their watchful eyes bearing down on me, making sure I did everything just right. If I made a mistake, they weren't very nice in the way that they let me know. Sometimes I would get so overwhelmed that I would leave the register, which was strictly forbidden by the company.

I was written up whenever I did it, and faced disciplinary action. I didn't want to lose my job, so I began looking for a solution to my challenges.

My college had a center for adults with autism called The Hussman Center, which provided a lot of resources, programs, and support to help people on the spectrum. Not only did they provide social group activities where like-minded individuals could connect, but they also provided guidance for common issues faced by adults on the spectrum. When I had trouble at my job, I turned to the center for advice. The director told me about federal laws that protect people with disabilities who are working, and that I could receive accommodations on the job. I filed the necessary paperwork, and my boss agreed to allow me additional breaks if I needed to step away to collect myself. Not all of the managers agreed with letting me have accommodations. They didn't know anything about autism, and to them it looked like I was slacking. Some of my co-workers became resentful towards me, because if I took an additional break it meant more work for them. One of my co-workers accused me of faking my disability so that I could get out of doing work. That was very hurtful. Spending every day at a job where I was looked down on for my disabilities and accommodations took a toll on my mental health, but thankfully I had The Hussman Center to turn to. Even though people at my job didn't know how to interact with me, the center gave me a safe haven where I could be with other people on the autism spectrum who would never judge me for my differences. We all had similar challenges, so we could relate to each other. The leaders of the program were all familiar with autism, and they were supportive and understanding. Having The Hussman Center in my life made it possible for me to thrive, even with all of the negativity I faced in the outside world. With their help I was able to get through my job, and earn enough money to pay for my final semester of college.

Graduation and grad school

There are no words for what it felt like to be graduating. A very small percentage of foster kids graduate, and an even smaller percentage of autistic foster kids graduate. With everything I had survived, I felt like I was one in a million. I had proven everyone who ever doubted me wrong. I have to admit, the prospect of graduating college boosted my ego. I wondered if I should stop there, or keep going. I felt grandiose in thinking that I might be able to go to grad school. Even the best of the "normal" students don't get accepted to grad school. But I hadn't gotten this far based on probabilities. If there was a possibility, I would go for it. I decided to apply to grad school. I thought about what kind of program I wanted to be in. I wanted to choose a field that would make me an easy shoe-in, a field where my uniqueness would be an asset. I had to find a school that did autism research, and had a high acceptance rate. A high acceptance rate doesn't exist for grad school, but I found a few universities that were easier to get into than others. I couldn't afford the application fees to apply to a lot of programs, so I chose three. I scavenged their websites, learning everything I could about their programs, and identified the professors who focused their research on autism. I contacted each one, introducing myself so that when my application arrived, they would already know who I was. I needed to stand out. Instead of focusing my goals statements on all of the clichéd traits that people list on résumés, I talked about my experiences as a person with autism who had a dream of helping other people with autism. I talked about the challenges that I faced, and how working with experts in the field of developmental psychology changed my life. I was hoping that they would read my statement, and see a living example of the epitome of why they chose to be in the field themselves. The more I worked on the applications, the more my aspiration of being a grad student grew. I became obsessed with it, and dreamed about how amazing it would be for someone like me to get in. Completing and submitting my applications was one of the most anxiety-provoking things I've ever done.

During the time that I waited to hear back from the grad schools, I had my undergraduate graduation. The night before the ceremony I cried and cried. I remembered the abused child who was made to think she was stupid and worthless, who had grown into an honors student. I reflected on the struggles I faced at my first college, and how much I doubted that I would ever succeed. I thought about the sliver of hope I had when I applied to my alma mater from a homeless shelter, and I remembered how much it crushed me to have my dream of being a teacher taken away. My day had finally arrived. All of the hell and hardship I survived was finally about to pay off. When I walked across the stage, and shook the dean's hand, I looked her in the eye. She could never know what this meant to me. I sent a kiss up to God, because sometimes my faith was the only thing that kept me alive, and I left the auditorium a college graduate.

About a month later I received my first rejection letter from one of the grad schools I had applied to. The second school didn't even send me a letter—they sent me an email notifying me of my rejection. I waited another month before hearing back from the final grad school. I was accepted! Just like when I got accepted as an undergraduate, I couldn't believe it. Instead of feeling overjoyed, I felt a wave of numbness wash over me. The feelings inside were so intense I couldn't even process them, and still to this day, I can't comprehend the fact that I got accepted. But here I am, now a second-year Master's student, studying developmental psychology. Despite all the odds I'm making it!

What helps?

When I look back at my troubles and triumphs, I have to say it was worth everything I went through. What helped me the most was having people who understood me, and who were willing to help me. They helped me obtain accommodations, and taught me how to advocate for myself. Learning how to seek help and talk to professors made a huge difference in whether or not I could survive my classes. I found that if professors had an understanding of my challenges, they were more likely to help me succeed. Accommodations were a necessity in eliminating challenges that would've otherwise destroyed my academic success. Without accommodations my performance didn't reflect my true capabilities; it reflected my disabilities. I think that all students with disabilities who are transitioning to college should be taught how to get the accommodations that they need, and how to advocate for themselves with professors. They should be prepared for the challenges of college life that are specific to their disability. For instance, I didn't know how stressful the social dynamic of dorm life would be, or how hard it would be to work in a group in class. I wish someone would have prepared me for how to deal with those situations. Also, where professional skills came somewhat naturally to my classmates, I was clueless on how to be professional. Colleges should develop support groups for people with disabilities that directly address their challenges as they relate to college success. People with disabilities shouldn't have to focus solely on their shortcomings. Interventions and support should be strengths-based, because strength builds confidence, and you need confidence to succeed. With support, understanding, and the right accommodations, I think anyone can succeed, regardless of their disability.

10

The Oops Baby

Dena L. Gassner, M.S.W.

I was born in 1958. Given that my brother is ten years older than me, and my sister is thirteen years older than me, it was pretty clear that I was "unplanned." However, like the good, logical (albeit undiagnosed) Aspie mom she was, my mother decided I should not grow up alone, and had a second child, two years after I was born.

My mother's family was part of the gypsy-like exodus of Appalachians who left the South (Alabama) to relocate to the Ohio Valley for factory work. She was one of six children who grew up in a family with two "jobs." My grandfather spent his days working in the refinery at Sohio Oil and his nights working his small tobacco farm. Each harvest, the kids would all come back to the farm and "put up tobacco." I only remember that process once since I was too little to work the farm, but I remember watching the adults, and it was back-breaking work to cut and hang the huge tobacco leaves to dry in the barn.

I remember very little of those days…most of my memories are a combination of actually literal snapshots from the photo album and mental snapshots, freeze-framed in my mind. While I don't recall it, I now know that this was a family filled with alcohol and domestic violence, in both my grandparent's generation and in the one that followed.

I recall only a few moments at the farm. There is one photo in our family album of me in red shorts with a white top with ruffled sleeves that had little red cherries on it; my Uncle Jimmy has his hand on my curly red head, and I am sitting in a box that I was using like a sled, going up and down the hills on the farm. I remember eating home-canned tangy pickled beets until I peed red. I remember eating homegrown tomatoes right off the vine like apples, and the juice running down my chin. I remember a beautiful fragrant plant with white flowers that we called a "snowball plant." I remember visiting with my grandparents at the VFW (Veterans of Foreign Wars) hall, and my mom asking me to hug Grandma, to which I bluntly replied, "No, she smells like beer and cigarettes." I remember harsh words and an unexpected slap to the face—one of only two times I was ever physically reprimanded by my mother. I remember sitting in my grandmother's living room while my mother talked to the police after her mother had committed suicide.

These memories are not fluid, or cohesive. They do not include conversations or relational experiences. They are held in my mind as isolated snapshots—not real memories—just like the white top with the ruffled sleeves and red cherries. The family system was so chaotic and unpredictable, and because there was so much chaos, my brain closed it all off.

My next real memory was the day the police came to get my little sister and me from my father's house. I've learned from my siblings that my mother experienced weekly—sometimes daily—domestic violence from my father. The day the police came was the day my mother left him. It was 1970; I was a first grader. I attended four schools between first and third grade, while my mother divorced, had an affair with her boss at the cocktail lounge/gambling establishment where she worked, and then married him. I don't remember when they actually got married. I just remember him being in the efficiency apartment over her work more and more often.

I have a few flash memories of that apartment. I remember wetting the bed and walking downstairs to the cocktail lounge to get my mom. Searching for her, I went to the back room and saw a round table with cards all over it surrounded by men. Smoke clouded my sleepy eyes. I was reprimanded for bothering her at work. There was the time I went to the bakery downstairs for bread and came home with nothing but a crust (how I loved, and still love, the gooey soft part inside a loaf of bread!). A boy in our neighborhood fell off a porch and hit his head. Another boy was scalded by water in his basement. My mother cracked me on the bottom for rubbing myself on the edge of the bed in front of my stepfather. I cried when I was made to stay after school. I had no way of knowing that I was academically advanced and that the teacher was keeping me to work on my math, possibly to promote me past a grade. That is a very clear memory. I experienced it as a traumatic event. But I smile because I remember seeing my baby sister waiting for me at the end of our block (we were two blocks from school and she was not allowed to cross the road). She so wanted to be in school, too, like her sissy.

At the beginning of the summer of my third grade year, we moved out of the city and into a tiny little two-bedroom rental house. It had a huge yard, was "safe," on a cul-de-sac, and was filled with rowdy little boys. I had long before denounced the pink aisle, but my sister had hoped for some girl power on the street. Soon I was running, playing, and hitting softballs with the best of them. Teddy (who had gotten all the "pink" between the two of us) spent most days with our cat, or puppy, and her Barbies, anxiously awaiting first grade.

Finally, her long-awaited first day came. She was so excited to be finally going to school! Then, on October 5, 1967, while crossing a street to get home, a car hit us. She died that afternoon. I was in a medically induced coma for ten days, during which time she was buried. My last memory of her was seeing her through an opening in the curtain, her tiny throat open, and filling it was a tracheotomy tube.

I was hospitalized for exactly 30 days, after which I was released, in a full body cast from my toes to my armpits. During those 30 days, my always-practical mom did what she thought was best.

While I had been in the hospital, she had a ritual where she sat with me from sun up until sun down each day, and then she went home and wiped out every sign of my baby sister. Our cheery yellow twin beds were gone, replaced with a full-sized, French provincial bed with a floral canopy. The green and yellow walls were painted pink and white. All images save two—the last Olan Mills (portrait) pictures of us both in summer shirts and the last image taken, of the two of us in the Easter dresses she had made us—were simply gone. Mom put that last photo on a table, with two angel candles on each side. Those ceramic angels were from the funeral and all she took with her from that day. Every other thing that had belonged to my sister was gone, save for a few tiny items stored in a large toy chest in the bathroom. Years later, my parents would go out for an evening and I would run to that box and carefully explore what she felt she needed to hold onto.

The sweet black patent leather Mary Jane's that she wore that day.

Lace-topped white socks.

A tiny white glove.

A Barbie.

And, the newspaper cuttings. As far as I could see, everything my hometown paper had printed had been carefully cut and saved. Over the years, the things she saved dwindled to a small game box. I still have that box.

The loss was different for me. I became very disconnected and introspective at that point. I believe I manifested many autism spectrum disorder (ASD) signs that were dismissed as the wild reworking of grief in a child's mind. I remember experiencing obsessive thinking, hyperlexia, idiosyncratic capacity for recall, and a natural and mature capacity for language beyond my years. I was a bit klutzy, chubby from overeating mostly carbs, and maintained a problem with making it to the bathroom due to hyperfocus when reading or engaged in television.

I was told that I began to play with my sister, like an imaginary friend, except she had existed. That's what triggered seeing a psychiatrist for the first time, at the age of nine. Although I don't quite recall a typical connection with my sister, I do recall having deep feelings of loss and loneliness. I had lost the support of my closest sibling. I often wonder who I might have become (good, bad, or indifferent) had my sister not left my world.

School

I survived my school career without a diagnosis or formal accommodations. Even with a diagnosis, I don't believe I would have benefited from many traditional supports like extended time or separate testing in the majority of my classes. With the exception of math challenges, academics were not difficult for me. However, in today's special education setting, I would have required the use of a calculator, a math fact sheet, and one-to-one remediation. I doubt that I would have passed a second year of Algebra. The issue was not basic math facts, but understanding and remembering math processes and sequences—challenges related to short-term and working memory issues of the perceptual issues—not the numbers themselves.

I would also have greatly benefited from support for organizing both smaller, daily assignments to consider the multitasking of shifting subjects, and for planning and organizing large, multistep tasks to spread them out over time.

Grade school

Academics have never been terribly difficult for me, except for math. Math began plaguing me back in second grade, when the teacher started keeping me after school. Today, I would have been diagnosed with a specific learning disability in math. But back then, my parents' attitude was, "Well, if you're doing so well in everything else, you must not be trying hard enough." Now, as an adult, I continue to have phobic reactivity in the face of numbers. My friend, Mary Robison, once described my math issues to include math phobia. So sad she passed on. I think she might have been the only one to understand the anxiety it created, and continues to create, for me.

Reading and writing were as easy as falling off a log. I was always bewildered by my peers' inability to read and write easily. And in a strange paradox, while my parents never supported the difficulty I had in math, they also never supported my gift for reading and writing. I believe part of it could have been that, like me, my mom was also a frenetic reader. Perhaps this was her "normal," so she thought nothing of it. For my stepfather, well, my educational needs and abilities would become part of a much darker scenario.

From the day he moved in, my stepfather was strict and withholding of affection or tenderness toward me. There had been some for my little sister, but he was controlling and demanding, as well as being unbearably strict, in a torturous, passive–aggressive manner. If I got 98 percent on a paper, he demanded that it should have been 100 percent. If I forgot to change out of school clothes, I was punished. Even if it meant that my mother would have to drive me to school, I could not leave without making my bed. Once he made me eat my breakfast out of the trash (I didn't want it, and "hid" it there).

When I could not memorize my multiplication tables, he forced me to sit at the kitchen table with him every day after school and drill with flash cards. The anticipation of that made me physically ill. It appeared that he was helping me, but it was one of many examples of behaviors that constituted grooming.

Middle school

At the end of my freshman year, I had my first decompensation (an episode in which a person with autism becomes completely overwhelmed with their life, or a specific circumstance that they are unable to continue to function; some wind up in psychiatric facilities, dropping out, stuck in bed, abandon work or relationships or, in the worst-case scenario, attempt or complete suicide).

During my freshman year of high school, I began to immerse and over-extend myself in after-school activities as a way to avoid being home. Starting in seventh grade, my stepfather began to act on the grooming protocol he had set in place, and he was touching me, and having me touch him; he was kissing me like a wife. He manipulated my mother into thinking that dressing me like an adult, in evening gowns, and taking me to supper clubs was giving me opportunities and experiences she had only dreamed of at my age. In reality, he was walking into high-end clubs frequented by his gambling pals (he was a bookie) with two young women (my mother looked younger than her age), and he loved it. It would be years before I would learn about psychological incest (using a child as a spouse) that was coupled with the physical assault. It would be even more years before I would have the capacity to say "no" to unwanted contact, or to be able to protect myself.

Also during this time, there was an assault from a much-older camp employee who became a minister, sexualized behaviors from another minister who attempted to meet up with me at a retreat, and a third minister who wrote me sexualized letters (I later learned that he had forced his wife to be part of that). The behaviors that my stepfather's grooming had created transferred into the church community I frequented as a teen, making me an easy, readily identifiable target. To this day, I don't know what behaviors I manifested to be marked as such, but targets are transparent to abusers.

Three days before the end of my freshman year, the cumulative impact of these assaults became too much to contain. I developed a migraine which mimicked the symptoms of a stroke. I lost the use of my left arm, and had word-finding as well as pronunciation issues. They had me call my mother and I was admitted into hospital, where it was thought that I could have a blood clot from the accident that was only then manifesting. In reality, I was having a decompensation.

Twenty-four hours later, the symptoms stopped, but they tested me for another five days. There was no medical cause. My mother asked what I thought had caused it, and I said, "You know what caused this. He did this." I had disclosed to my mother about the abuse from her husband on this, the third, occasion, but she could not reconcile that the man who had rescued her from her abuser could also be my abuser. She never acknowledged it. Neither did he. They exempted me from finals, and in August, I began my high school experience.

High school

I marched in the high school band and sang in the choir as a means to meet and make friends. Being involved in the band in high school integrated me with my peers, and while I was always very social (I'm rather an extrovert on steroids, blowing the introvert Aspie profile), I do recall a feeling of isolation and loneliness, a separateness that's still difficult to describe. My participation in school events resulted in out-of-town trips and after-school events that my stepfather insisted I didn't "have" to do. It was more of his control. But the sexual assaults stopped.

The only academic wall I hit, other than a continuation of the math difficulties, was Spanish class. I suspect it was more of that same working memory problem rather than actual language per se. I am shocked at how much of it I recall, but the class moved too quickly for me. Also, the teacher was not easy to work with. My mother made the one and only appearance at my school, and had me withdrawn.

At the end of my junior year, I noticed some friends had skipped their senior year. Friends had all applied to colleges and had options. I had no overall conception of planning my future.

College

The only person who suggested college for me was my church pastor, who had left our church to become the campus minister of Union College, a small United Methodist-affiliated college in southeast Kentucky. I have no idea exactly how I got in. I have no memory of applications, financial aid, or any other details, and since I was the first in my family to attend college, there was no help from home.

The only action I remember taking for college was how sad my scores in math were. I had a 12 in math, but in comparison, a 16 in language and an 18 in science. My math was so tragically low that my enrollment was conditional on me passing a non-credited basic math class in the first semester. Fortunately, I never had to take another math class again.

As an aside, I firmly believe that unless you are in a math-dependent area of study (science, medicine), math mandates are not useful. From my position, functional, daily math involving banking, personal budgets, and other essential math competencies seem more relevant.

At the end of my summer jobs, I never had any money to show for my efforts. I received no direct instruction to learn about money management. My mother did not give me an allowance but just what I needed, when I needed it. When I left for college, I had several hundred dollars in my bank account, but within a week, it was depleted.

As a 56-year-old adult, I have found that using cash and writing money orders keeps me from spending "invisible" money—things related to a checking account like "float," or the time discrepancy between money spent and money withdrawn from one's account. Sometimes there are hours, days in the case of international circumstances, weeks even between when money is spent and when that cash is taken from the account. As you can see, I fully understand the process—it's the implementation that is ineffective. However, if you use cash or money orders, there is no float. The identified balance on the ATM card is what is actually in the account. Wow, I wish my younger self had known about simpler strategies! When I pay my bills with money orders, and use cash, the money is concrete and physical. Paying with checks has always been problematic. All to say, whatever works, works. We don't have to do everything the way others do.

Small academic accommodations were informally provided, such as extended time for me when I had too many deadlines, and on two occasions, my professor allowed me to retake a test because I panicked in two or three random situations. Given my difficulties with multitasking the varying and increasing deadlines near the end of each term, I would inevitably run out of time. There were two or three professors during my undergraduate days who would intervene if I hit those kinds of walls.

I was also fortunate to be a "big fish in a small pond" by attending a very small private, church-affiliated college. A state university would have eaten me alive. This school allowed me to grow, strive, and be fully integrated far more successfully than I had been in high school. It was a relatively safe place to make the huge mistakes I made. I continue to have remarkable friendships that have stood the test of time, all starting at that tiny little school.

Finally, in the spirit of full disclosure, I will acknowledge that I engaged in the use of marijuana to maintain sensory and emotional regulation during college. I had not engaged in the use of illegal drugs during high school, and I found that alcohol had too many negative side effects. However, pot quieted my noisy brain, allowed me to sleep, and disinhibited much of my anxiety. The down side was that it disinhibited my behavior at times in such a way as to place me at risk; however, the very small campus and rural area were, in themselves, somewhat of a protection. Simply put, it limited the amount of exposure to serious problems that could happen. Still, there are some decisions that happened during college and later, after I was married the first time, that I wish I could change.

Graduate school

I married twice. Once to the father of my children, and then again, when the children were seven and four. It was during my second marriage that I decided to return to college for my graduate degree.

After my son, Patrick (also a contributing author here) was diagnosed with autism, I decided to leave my first career in property management for social work. When he was three, I returned to graduate school to study social work. In my undergraduate studies, I majored in humanities. However, I returned to graduate school nearly 20 years after finishing my undergraduate studies with only one class in human services (psychology 101). I had two children—one, eight, with autism and one, twelve, with attention deficit hyperactivity disorder (ADHD)—who never slept.

The only intervention I had was the support of one of my much-loved professors during a terribly dark moment. During an internship, one of my site supervisors targeted me for workplace harassment. It was subtle, insidious, and terribly persistent. She left papers in my office suggesting that I should not be a social worker. I complained, but I was the one who paid a price. Despite completing over 700 hours of training under her supervision, she failed me. It was the only "F" I ever received in 14 years of education. My professor sensed the discordant attitudes she exhibited, and offset her "F" with an "A." It remains one of my most shameful and frustrating experiences—particularly since it occurred at a facility charged to diagnose children with developmental disabilities.

Some years later, I learned that she continued to demonstrate these behaviors toward one student each semester, and first, lost supervision privileges, and ultimately, her position. Ten years later the program sent out a survey. I refused to respond because it disallowed one to express anything other than "yes" or "no." I most certainly wanted to say more than whether or not my training had taught me anything. It taught me more. I learned that I should never dismiss my intuition. My intuition told me that she was a dark person. I wanted the training so badly that I disregarded the bad feelings I felt in her company. I learned that men were not the only people to be cautious about. I learned that women, too, are, at times not trustworthy.

It was then—during these dark days—that I learned that like, yet unlike, my son, I, too, live with autism. My manifestation is not as recognizable as his. Upon meeting me, one is unlikely to realize that I am autistic.

The words that have been used by people to describe me include: autistic, intense, focused, generous, passionate, bossy, demanding, persistent, and unrelenting.

But once I understood autism, my autism best described my unique personality. It took me over ten years to detox from the medications that maltreated me for conditions I did not have, and to integrate the diagnosis, working and reworking my past until I understood the implications of my autism in all of my trials and difficulties. It was the reason for my vulnerability. It was the reason I demonstrated sexualized behaviors without understanding the implications. It was the reason I was so fragile, yet so intense. It explained the dichotomies of learning I had experienced. It explained who I was, not only to others, but also most importantly, to myself.

From that point on, I stopped trying to outgrow my difference, and learned the very important benefits of growing into my condition. I am now a whole being, with all the hidden parts now visible. With that knowledge of self, I have grown into the most complete expression of myself possible to date, to the peak of my authenticity.

Adulthood

At reunions, my classmates insisted that they saw no signs of disability when we were in school together. Still, in recollection, I realize that save two specific girls, I don't recall doing anything with girlfriends. I participated in many group events, like skating or church activities, but I wasn't personally invited to do many things at all.

So many kids with ASDs express that they "feel different" and think, "everyone knows I'm weird." I'd say that was my experience, too, but it was very ethereal and intangible during my school days. I was very disconnected from self, and while I feel more connected to self than ever before, even now that "outsider" feeling still exists.

A few wonderful days per year, I get to spend time surrounded by other people with autism. I see a new generation of sweet young people creating their own community. Content, despite their uniquely effortful journeys, these young people are the new faces of autism. They don't have to wait until they are 38 or 40 or 60 to learn who they are. They were empowered by the gift of diagnosis and the integration that knowledge gives.

They look to each other, and their elders, for the growth and learning to be the best they can.

Still, there are people "out there" surrounded by often well-intentioned parents/educators/providers who dismiss these feelings of being outside by expressing that the person is "wonderful" and "being silly" and "everyone loves you," but it does not help the individual to find language to explain this to themselves as well as to others. They need legitimate validation that they are, in fact, different; they need to understand it in a meaningful, proactive way.

Because I was not diagnosed until adulthood, my parents didn't provide any transition training, support, or even the understanding of the need for this. I was very verbal prompt-dependent. I see this quite often in the clients I work with now. Verbal reminders create a person-dependent student. Instead, creating charts, calendars, or lists for the wall or the phone is so helpful. These are portable systems that go with the individual and are critically needed.

While in high school I worked at a camp during the summer. My clothes all mildewed because I didn't understand, functionally, how to do laundry. I worked in the kitchen and was tormented by my boss for licking my fingers while cooking. I'd only ever cooked in my house, where that was normal. A pair of rubber gloves could have disrupted the behavior. Instead of this being a good, independent living, vocational experience, I felt persecuted and functioned to simply avoid ridicule rather than positively working toward personal skills.

The sexual abuse I experienced may have been averted had I understood not only functional skills, but also basic safety and boundary training. Simply knowing the "rule" to never be alone with someone of the opposite sex could have changed my life.

With my kids, I did it differently. When my daughter and son reached the developmental age of 14 (she was on time; he was not there until the chronological age of around 18), I began giving them $100 a month at the beginning of each month. I told them what I would continue to support (prom expenses, clothes in the Fall/Spring, soap and shampoo, food at home, movies, games, and when we went out together as a family) and what I would not (activities/meals without the family, clothes in between seasons, cosmetics, etc.). Then I told them they had to make it last. Now my daughter has a six-month emergency fund, a three-bedroom house and an IRA (individual retirement account), a wife, a son, and a solid university position.

My son, who's still in college, always has pocket money at the end of each month, and purchases all the gifts for family members, as well as his eating out money. This year, his junior year at Marshall, he has moved into his own apartment.

Many people around the transitioning individual can make the mistake of presuming that factual knowledge can spontaneously transition real life, or that the person knows much more than they do. As you can see, this is a dangerous and risky presumption to make. I was fortunate, but many are not so lucky.

When I think of my first day on campus, it's as though I am right there, in my dorm room again. I am sitting on the side of my bed, tears streaming down my face. I. Was. Terrified. I found myself talking to the frightened little girl, out loud.

"It's not going to get better sitting here. Go outside. Meet someone."

And I did.

Now I am again in graduate school. At age 56, I've returned for my doctorate at Adelphi University. But this person is not that frightened little girl. That person is a work in progress, but still, an integrated, authentic voice on campus. I'm still exploding The Box (as in "outside the box"). I am living in dorms with undergraduates! But I am there, present, and soaking in every moment, armed with my self-awareness and the accommodations that affords.

My wish list for what I would have wanted is brief. I wish:

» I had been diagnosed and helped through integrating my new understanding before leaving for college. The lack of self-connection negatively impacted me all through my life, and continues to challenge me. It cost me the relationship of my life, and I still grieve that loss.

» I would have understood fully that what was happening in college would determine whether I was employed or not. Honestly, I had no idea. It just seemed like a "next step" to me, completely disconnected from career or income.

» I'd been provided the therapy to know how to handle myself as a sexual person. My risk-taking behaviors also took a huge toll on my self-esteem and personal wellness.

» I'd had the medication intervention I needed so that I would not have sought self-medication as it was not regulated and resulted in poor decision-making, also with negative outcomes.

» I'd been more fully celebrated and loved, as is, without condition. While I've learned that those feelings actually come from within, it is cultured and nurtured from the soil of one's inner child, and my child was badly bruised by so many losses and such bewilderment about self.

I would NOT change:

» The natural, relationship-based supports I got all on my own, without a diagnosis or a disability services protocol. Dr. Finkel and Dr. Judy Jennings empowered me just because. It was wonderful.

» My intense involvement in musical theater at school. It is the people I performed with who continue to be the foundation of long-term relationships in my world to this day. The theater rehearsal responsibilities created blocks of mandatory performance academically. Knowing I could not study after 6pm because of rehearsals gave me the external structure I could not create for myself.

» Attending a small school. There was a community there that is difficult to reproduce today.

» No television, DVD players, Xboxes, or cell phones. This forced us to get out of our rooms and into the student center where we learned about each other and loved one another!

I have no regrets. College was a step toward autonomy. I encourage you to read my son, Patrick Kelty's, story—his autism profile is quite different from mine. Not to mention that he had a diagnosis at age three, and parents who always let him know he was loved.

All to say, the outcomes for people with autism today are more than accommodations and supports. It's about finding one's authentic and unique identity, and using that as a foundation to fuel the flames of desire to succeed and to be individually successful, however that's defined. It matters not how long it takes. It matters not how much help it takes. All that matters is that you utilize whatever supports you can in continuing in your lifelong journey to wholeness, wellness, and achievement.

11

My Best Decision Ever

Patrick Kelty, Marshall University, West Virginia

My name is Patrick Kelty and I am a junior at Marshall University. Getting to Marshall was a dream come true, but it was not an easy journey.

The early days

I was diagnosed with autism at the age of three. It was not Asperger's syndrome, but classic autism. I have been told that they thought my IQ (intelligence quotient) was very low, and I had trouble getting my body and mind to work together, so I was delayed in many ways. I had a lot of sensory issues, and everything was too loud, too bright, too fast for me. The doctor told my mom about my autism like it was terrible. He said, "I'm very sorry to tell you." but she did not listen to him. She just did whatever it took to help me achieve.

I am the only boy in a combined family of four children. I have an older sister three years older than I, a stepsister just a few months younger, and a baby sister who is seven years younger. I was raised by my mom and my stepfather, Rick.

In the early days, my mom took me to speech therapy and sensory therapy up to four times a week. She talked to me all the time to help me develop language, and even though I didn't speak much, she never thought or acted like I wasn't able to understand. She said we tried some medications, but they only made everything worse.

Elementary school

Mom said it took her a long time to realize that people were not going to want to help me. I needed a lot of help to learn, and instead of giving me accommodations, teachers just assumed I could not learn.

My first school was set up for 100 kids in each classroom, and I quickly got overwhelmed. One of my first goals was to sit in a chair, but the room was so big, and I felt so lost, that the only way I could feel my body was to be on the floor. By the end of kindergarten, I had a one-to-one support person.

By third grade I began to have seizures. The noise, motion, and activity in the large room overwhelmed me. My mom knew I needed a different environment, and fought to get the district to move me to a traditional smaller classroom.

First, the school with the giant rooms created a traditional classroom that was designed to hold 25 students or so. But these students were not learning academics, and they had behaviors that were startling to me. I don't say that to be mean. It was just that it was unpredictable and terrifying when someone would let go a blood-curdling scream. I knew they could not help it, but it was hard for me.

Every day, my mom had to carry me in, and I cried most of the day because I wanted to be included. I didn't like not learning. So she got me into a different community school and I finally had a teacher who was willing to help me learn.

I made the honor roll in the first year! My teacher wrote down my words for me, and expected me to learn and participate. I even did a school musical and gave a speech. But after that, I had the same kind of teachers who didn't know how to teach me, and they put the blame on me, telling each other that I just could not learn.

Middle school

Middle school was a big issue. My mom saw kids pretend to high-five me and pull away, and other mean boy things. My special education teacher dragged me around with him all day, and I was not learning. My mom observed, and in one class my desk didn't even face the teacher.

The last straw was when a student assaulted me within the second month. I was shoved into the corner of a table, getting a huge bruise. My words would not work and no one knew how bad it was [the bruise was baseball-sized] until my mom saw it when I got home. The school tried to cover it up because the room had been left unattended by a principal. My mom was not going to let me not be safe, so I went to a small private school for special needs students for two years.

The private school was quieter and calmer, with only six or seven students per class. I learned to use a keyboard, to stay on topic, and to work at being focused in class, and that has helped me all my life. But even at this school, the teachers didn't expect learning for college for us, so we made a big decision and left my community behind to try school in North Carolina.

North Carolina

North Carolina schools turned out to be worse than my Kentucky and Ohio schools. In seventh grade, my friend with autism was maced by the school resource officer and he wasn't even doing anything. That frightened me.

Another day, a student asked me to toss him a book, and then he lied and pretended I had hit him on the head. He wanted to get out of class. All I could say was, "I didn't do it" over and over again. I kept saying it all day. Finally, at 2pm they called my mom in, and with her there, I could say more. Even though they learned that I had not done it, no one apologized to me for accusing me of lying.

The worst was when the teachers pushed me from sixth grade to eighth, skipping seventh altogether. Then, in eighth grade, they stopped helping me. They wanted me to fail so they could take away my help for other students. They didn't want to give me as much help as I needed, and they wanted an excuse to take away my option to complete a diploma.

The worst days were when a teacher who had gotten in trouble from what he said in a meeting closed me off in a classroom with another teacher who was his witness, and he threatened me. He said, "Don't you go home tellin' your mama all about school" and other evil things. He would stop me in the hallway and say, "You gonna call your mama?" It was very scary and I was even afraid to walk my dog alone at night. I always thought he would be there. Even after I moved to Tennessee, and we came back to North Carolina to do testing, I was afraid he would know I was there. My psychologist and therapist who were my advocates were even frightened. It was terrible. But I did not give up on my learning. Even when they didn't help me to show my abilities, I kept soaking it in. I knew someday I would succeed.

All of this conflict was really because the school didn't want to give me the accommodations I needed to learn. Even though I was diagnosed with autism when I was three, it was not autism that made learning hard. I was not diagnosed with multiple learning disabilities until I was a freshman in high school. Because of that, for the first ten years of school, people assumed I was not able to learn or go to college, so the school people thought I was a waste of their time.

The accommodations I needed were a note-taker, someone to write down my words (a scribe), a computer, a reading system that would read out loud to me, and someone to help with organizing my work. Then they decided, without my mom's permission, to stop letting me try for my diploma. That's when we moved to Tennessee, where I exploded with learning!

Tennessee

The teachers and students in Tennessee believed in me! On the first Friday at my new school, I wrote that "Even the ladies in the cafeteria are nice!" I went to a high school that was filled with students who were taught to include kids like me, and they spoke to me all the time. There were teachers who knew how to help me show that I was learning. I had someone write for me (even in math!) and take notes for me so I could focus on listening only. They also helped me with getting all my assignments organized and finished on time.

When I got to high school, I really could not read. Until I got to high school, there was no special intervention to help me read. The truth is, they thought I was too autistic to learn it.

I knew some words by sight and memorization, but actually reading and breaking down unfamiliar words was not possible. I never read for fun. So, after I got to high school, because everything was going well, I had the energy to attend tutoring to try to help me with reading.

I started with a private tutor who helped me learn more about how to sound out a word for real reading using a program called the Wilson Reading System (WRS). [Wilson helps with decoding and phonemic awareness.] It was very hard because I don't hear things the way other people do [auditory processing dysfunction is when the hearing and the processing do not work in sync]. WRS is all about sounding words out. But I persisted.

After that summer, my tutor, Mrs. Tiffany Anderson, came to school to get them to do Wilson Reading with me. She thought I needed it four days a week, and she could only see me for two (the tutoring center was 50 miles away, round trip). I tried with them for a while, but Mrs. Tiffany kept finding mistakes in their teaching. She came back to the school to advocate for me to have her do all of my instruction in WRS, and we won! So, for two full school years and three more summers, I worked to learn to read correctly.

During that catch-up time, I also needed to keep up with my classes. Since I could not read at grade level, but could understand if it was read out loud, I tried reading software that was supposed to read out loud to me. It was called Kurzweil. But the school never really got the Kurzweil up and running. I mostly stayed caught up with my peers by my teachers reading the material to me out loud and some books on tape. It was very hard.

I also had all my tests read aloud to me. I had multiple-choice tests, and that was very important. If I have to find a word in my head, it's confusing. But if I see the word, I can identify the right answer. [Word-finding skills, or word retrieval, is often very challenging for people with autism spectrum disorders (ASDs) and learning disabilities.] Working memory, or the capacity to keep the concepts in mind while producing a written document, is often difficult as well. Fill in the blanks, choices with multiple short-answer options, matching, multiple choice, these are all are forms of testing and evaluation that do not depend on word retrieval or working memory.) The teachers took extra time for me to get my assignments done. They were wonderful!

The best part of high school was managing the hockey team. I became part of something. I was the hydration consultant. I had filled over 900 water bottles by the end of my fourth year. I only had two small bullying experiences at this high school, and it was my hockey team brothers who had my back. For the first time, other students stood up for me. They were not huge things, like in North Carolina, but the teachers didn't even get involved. It was a brotherhood, and I learned about being part of a championship team. All the guys and their girlfriends came to my birthday parties, and I danced with the girls at homecoming and prom. I will never forget those days.

I finished all my courses, and I graduated with a 3.1 grade point. We did not know until we got to my seat and there was a paper certifying that I was a Tennessee honors diploma winner! It wasn't easy, but it was the most wonderful four years of my education to that point.

Also during high school, my mom was helping me with working on the skills you need to survive that do not have anything to do with classes. These skills are called life skills. By the time I got to high school, I had already learned many things, like how to make sure I had my wallet, keys, and cell phone (there was a dry erase board by the front door for a year, with the written prompt to "Remember the Three"). I had learned to cook a couple of meals. I had a schedule to remember when to shower and shave, and I used my cell phone as my alarm. [Patrick had another visual schedule in his room that identified those nights. But it was time for me to learn the confidence in those skills. So, in my sophomore year, my mom took a job teaching people about autism that made it so she had to travel all over the country. She was gone twice a month, for three days each trip. And I had to live on my own!

At first, friends from my church youth group or the hockey team would come over, after school, and spend the night. The hockey coaches and players helped me get to practice. Then my friends started just coming when it was time for bed (making it so I had to cook and get ready for school on my own, but they were there to check on me, and to make sure I didn't miss the bus—my greatest fear of all!). Then I started staying on my own. It was a gradual process and a little scary, but it was great practice for me, for when I did leave for college.

So that was it. I owe a lot to my fourth grade teacher who never gave up on me. I owe a lot to the school psychologist in North Carolina who was angry at how I was treated, and helped me by encouraging the school in Tennessee to give me a chance. I started to learn to read with Mrs. Tiffany. Mr. Kevin Vaughn helped me make it through Algebra and learning how to take tests. I owe everything about my personality to my Centennial teachers, my church friends in Franklin, and the Centennial Cougar championship winners who taught me brotherhood, and because of the Cougars, my name is engraved on a trophy. That is the best!

College

College was not part of the plan in my early years. Learning was so hard, the teachers did not believe in me, and many did not want to help me. My high school teachers saved me, and gave me ways to show that all along, I had been learning.

Even though we never thought it would happen, or even could happen, college was always something I wanted to do, just like all three of my sisters. After graduation I went to a college for students with learning disabilities in Florida. It was really small, so my mom thought they would give me the same kind of support I had had in high school, but they didn't. After one Summer term and the first Fall term (15 hours), I came back home. It was sad for me because they wouldn't help me, but I saw them helping others. It was a very hard time for us, and it was looking like college was not going to happen.

Then I considered two other college programs closer to our home in Tennessee. The first would not even interview me because of my anxiety, though.

The second, well, the ladies there didn't understand me. They both wanted me to be able to talk to them, but their questions were too wide, and they wanted me to use word-finding instead of word choices. [One of the greatest difficulties for students with ASDs is the college interview. In our opinion, not adapting the interview to the needs of the student creates a barrier that is unreasonable as it directly challenges their most impacting skills—social competency and verbal expression—and it is not the best measure of a student's academic capabilities. It's like asking a student who uses a wheelchair to stop being disabled and to walk for an interview. Also, the interviewers are often ineffective in knowing how to secure information from the student with the least amount of anxiety—the deal breaker. This team was ineffective.]

I didn't like having to sit facing them or being closed off in an office. It reminded me of North Carolina. [They had been informed in advance of Patrick's fear of closed offices and past trauma in that setting.] The women were rushed and made me feel pressured.

Their questions were [abstract] too wide, like "Why do you want to go to college?" And "What will you do if you have a problem?" How can I know what I will do when I don't know the problem? [This was very frustrating as we asked for the interview to be accommodated by doing a walking interview, outside of the office, and that they weigh Patrick's grades and a video character reference higher. We articulated expressive language and word-finding difficulties that are escalated in pressured settings, yet they were inflexible. Not a good first sign.] Near the end, they said, "You know, when you get to college, your mom can't help you anymore." That was the last straw. I walked out. It was a bad day for us.

Then I got the chance to be interviewed for the College Program for Students with Autism at Marshall University. Marshall had always been at the top of our list, but since they only take ten students per year, we were sure it would be too hard for me to get in. But we were out of options, and so they saw me anyway.

The interview at the Marshall College Program was very different. They agreed not to take me into an office. We met in an open space with comfy chairs that people hang out in during school, and I didn't have to face anyone. The people knew what to do when I got anxious. They stopped asking me wide questions and asked me instead about the movie I brought to show them. They didn't really ask about college much at all. [Dr. Marc Ellison, Interim Director of the Marshall Autism Training Program, explained that their primary objective was not to conduct an interview, per se, but to chat. He wanted to measure Patrick's anxiety and to see if, when talking about subjects of interest, the anxiety could be regulated. Patrick regulated, shared, chatted, and performed beautifully.]

After the interview, my mom drove me to the cemetery where the remains of the 1970 Marshall Thundering Herd football team members and boosters (fans and parent supporters) were buried. There, I touched the monument with the names of those who had perished. We also visited the fountain on campus that is another memorial to them. And I prayed that I would be a member of the Herd.

Despite how well my interview went, I still had to be accepted by the Marshall admissions department. At first, I was not accepted. I was really upset and spent a lot of time listening to my Pokémon soundtracks. They were very positive, and the lyrics spoke to me about courage and believing in yourself.

Then the College Program people told me to write an appeal letter, and to tell them why things had gone wrong in Florida, and how I would work to make that different. They also told me to tell them that that I *was* accepted to the College Program, so the admissions people would know I would not be alone.

I wrote an appeal letter explaining why I had trouble with the requirements (my ACT scores were low because I didn't perform well on standardized tests, but my grades showed that I could learn). I explained about my learning problems, and that the first program I tried had staff that didn't understand how to work with me, or have the time.

I also explained about my emotional connection to Marshall. I told them that I could identify with the town and the campus. Like them, I also had to overcome great hardships to succeed. Like them, my first time trying to come back wasn't as good as I had hoped. But I didn't stop trying.

I explained that this was just like the town of Huntington that had overcome their losses. It was like how Marshall's students and campus had to overcome the tragedy when the plane crash happened in '70. I told them I could feel their courage when I stood at the fountain that "mourns the lost." I explained that, like Marshall, I could "rise from the ashes."

We all danced the day my acceptance letter arrived. I kept it in a frame in my dorm room to remind me about not giving up. Now it hangs in my apartment off-campus, where I live alone, using many of the independent living skills that I learned so long ago, from the hockey players and youth group leaders.

Day one at Marshall

The first thing we needed to do was to figure out who was going to help me and how. There was another meeting, with the learning disabilities people, the disability services office, and the College Program. We had some trouble because the other two offices started with those open questions again, like, "What do you think you will need?" Seeing my panic, Mrs. Rebecca Hansen of the College Program came to my rescue! She started asking me questions in a different way, so I could answer using choices instead of word-finding. With her help, we decided I would try different things. Some are common to most college disability services programs, and some things are exceptional and usually only provided by autism support programs. I will show the different ones:

» Note-takers in every class who took notes with my laptop—I can't read cursive, so this was important.

» Tutors for math and science (I tried the commonly offered tutors provided by disabilities services; however, I needed someone trained to work with challenged learners, so the College Program helped find and train the tutors themselves, which is very uncommon, even at most college autism programs).

The commonly offered accommodations that helped me were:

» Digital textbooks readable by my Kurzweil.

» Separate testing in the College Program offices.

» Flexible scheduling if I had more than one exam on the same day.

» Two hours a week in the writing center to work on editing of writing work.

» A letter from disability services stating that I am registered in the program, and what accommodations I receive.

» Accommodations for food sensitivities from the dining services people.

Then, I learned that the College Program would provide other supports that went farther than just disability services (uncommonly offered, but provided for my individual needs through the program):

» A descriptive, two-page letter, written together with my mom, that explained how my autism looks in a classroom. They needed to know things like I don't talk a lot, I may not look like I am participating but I am, and when I do talk, it sometimes isn't on topic. I think it helps them to understand me better.

» Registration and withdrawals from classes, as needed.

» A weekly meeting on Monday, where I get a spreadsheet schedule.

» Communication or "translator services" if my grades aren't posted or some conversation needs to happen to explain them to me.

» Negotiation with other student departments when I needed help, like with housing and disability services.

» Transition of laundry skills to dorm laundry (I could do laundry, but it's different when you use a card to pay and have to hang out with it instead of watching movies or reading).

» Transportation training to the movies, shopping, and places I want to go.

» Help making sure all my books are digitized and usable by my Kurzweil. The staff even got trained on Kurzweil so they could help me and other students.

Vocational Rehabilitation is a state agency that helps train people with disabilities for jobs. They helped, too. They provided:

» books

» fees for the College Program

» tuition

» a computer

» Kurzweil software.

They also paid for my Irlen lenses. I first got them in third grade when I was having seizures, and they stopped them—the lenses filter out the colors in light waves that cause me to see distortions and make me feel sick.

Some life skills accommodations were needed too. Simplify was the key word. All my socks are the same and match. All my clothes in my first year were light colored (now I can sort the lights and darks). My mother painted red lines with nail polish on the shower so I would not burn myself if I could not set the water temperature. Now that I am in my own apartment, she's done the same to the stove and the dishwasher, to help with the settings.

I have low muscle tone in my hands, so cleaning is hard. So my stepdad and my mom come to campus once a month to clean my apartment.

Another important contributor, and the most important person for my academics, is my tutor, Kenny, who helps me organize my work and know what to do. If you ask me, "Patrick, what do you need to do today?" my organizing system will not let me say. I can't recognize what I need to do that way. But if you assign me jobs, I can do them and I never miss a deadline. Kenny assigns me tasks and breaks the work down into jobs so I can do them. That is something programs don't provide, so my mom had to hire him privately and Vocational Rehabilitation pays for him.

Something no one would have predicted happened, too. Last summer, something clicked. I think it was all the reading intervention combined with the Kurzweil working well at Marshall, but I have become a person who reads for happiness! I have read nearly every day for six months now, and I love it! I collect books along with my movies, and my room is too small for them all, but it's been the best gift ever.

None of this would have happened without my mom and stepdad, Rick. This Fall, they helped me move into my own apartment, off-campus. This is a big step in my independence, and I could not have done it without them.

One other very best part of being part of Marshall—I met coach Red Dawson. After seeing him in the movie, "We Are

Marshall," he's my friend now. I tailgate with him and have met Reggie Oliver who was the first quarterback after the plane crash. Red and his friends often have lunch with me during the week.

I also had the honor of being the first student from the College Program to lay a rose at the memorial fountain at the memorial ceremony we have every year to honor the football team. I take flowers to the cemetery at the end of every semester because I believe the team from the crash supports me and gives me courage each day. Marshall uses a phrase in their billboards— "Best. Decision. Ever." Marshall was for me.

12

College Dreams

Kerry Magro

There are many books out there today which discuss the topic of how to get into and graduate from college, but I feel there are not enough focused on getting through college with a disability. This is where I think my story may come in handy.

Most know me today as a national speaker, best-selling author, and award-winning disability advocate. These efforts started out because of my college experiences. This was the first time I came out to my peers about my diagnosis with autism. It was while I was in college that my advocating not only started, but progressed along two different paths:

» advocating to help myself get through school and

» advocating to help others do the same.

When I was four years old I was diagnosed with pervasive developmental disorder—not otherwise specified (PDD-NOS), a form of autism. I had countless difficulties to overcome. One of the first signs started a year-and-a-half before the diagnosis, when at two-and-a-half I was still non-verbal. I was an only child, and everyone said just a later bloomer, but at two-and-a-half, it was becoming a concern. By four I had some delayed speech, but getting the diagnosis of autism, which is essentially a communication disorder, made it easier to understand why this was happening to me, but it did not make it any less challenging for me to keep up with my peers when it came to communication.

My parents took this diagnosis and then went on the offensive, getting me involved with intense physical, occupational, speech, and social therapy. These therapies were happening the same time I was beginning pre-kindergarten, so my schedule was quickly filling up. During this transition I had begun to have more and more emotional issues. Between a lack of social communication and adjustment difficulties, my parents thought I might have had an emotional disorder. I had already been kicked out of two pre-schools by this time, both schools saying they couldn't control me. I received a confirming re-diagnosis a year later, at age five, and two years ago, at age 23, when I graduated college, that I had PDD-NOS.

The re-diagnosis was something that struck a chord with my parents because it gave them some much-needed closure. After additional tests, they knew where I was, and were looking apprehensively towards the future without much to go on. The transition to therapeutic pre-kindergarten was not easy. They dropped me off every morning and I would scream and kick the door. After months in a multihandicapped class, I made it through kindergarten mostly unscathed thanks to an amazing teacher, Barbara Balsamo. Grammar school opened up a large amount of complications all around transitioning. At the age of six, in 1994, special education classes for students in public schools dealing with my diagnoses were still largely in development in my hometown of Jersey City, New Jersey.

One of the first transition issues early on involved getting my therapies. During first grade the consulting therapists for our class for occupational and physical therapy deemed the school that we were attending was too "dangerous," and therefore would not provide therapy as long as we attended that school. This resulted in our entire special education class being moved to another school across town for second grade, which involved transitioning, and which ended up not working out for me as well. By third grade it was yet another move to a different school in another part of town where we thought we had a solution with a highly sought-after special needs teacher who was highly recommended at a school farther from my house. Within weeks of starting third grade there, my parents were told that, due to being pregnant, the teacher had decided to take maternity leave. I remained there for the next two years, at a school with 1200 kids where bullying was a critical concern for me. My parents removed me under the unilateral placement of student's provision to go out of district while we navigated the New Jersey state due process system. The bottom line was that my parents, like millions of parents advocating for their children, sued the school system on my behalf. My situation was furthered complicated by the fact that my mother, who ran for the education board to help me in 1996, was now president of the board of Jersey City Education, and was essentially suing herself. Nothing ever seemed to come easy in this process, and my mom wounded up having to take a second job and drive me two hours minimum a day to Teaneck, New Jersey, for eight years, to make sure I was in the right place. That probably made the difference between where I would have been and where I am today. For my entire middle school experience (from fifth to eighth grade) I attended Community School in Teaneck, New Jersey, for students with learning disabilities.

During my middle school experience, everything changed for the better for me. I had finally gone to an environment where I was accepted for who I was. Every student in our school of only 160 kids was on the same playing field with one another. Everyone knew they had something, a disability that made them unique, and no one went out of their way (for the most part) to do anything other than treat each other with respect. My grades were able to flourish, and even though I had some difficulties with emotional issues, I finally had some place I could form a much-needed routine in. Also, every teacher was trained in special education, and we had a comprehensive behavior modification system, including a reward system and gold card system for good behavior.

Four years later my parents applied for me to local magnet schools at the Jersey City and Hudson County level. Though they didn't tell me, none of them accepted me because they assumed I either couldn't do it, fit in, or couldn't handle the curriculum. So for me, the transition to high school was one of the simplest I've had in school. My parents just told me I was staying at Community School for high school. The out-of-district grammar school I attended had a joint high school program! The high school, like the grammar school, only had 160 students, and almost all the students I graduated with went to high school with me. It was literally across the street from the grammar school, and shared the Fields of Dreams outdoor fields that had recently been developed by the joint capital program between the schools. Things were looking up immediately.

To summarize my high school experience, I would say that it was the prologue to my eventual self-advocacy work. I was at this time beginning to pick up on my communication a bit more, and had started becoming more social. Because I was working less on my therapies now I had more time to spend on focusing on my key interests. One of those interests was basketball. I had always had a fascination in watching basketball, and wanted to take that interest into competing in it. When I found out that there was a basketball team at high school (unlike our grammar school), I was sold.

A major deficit I had making this a reality, though, was that I was trying to work on my weight. I started as a high school freshman being 5'11" and 230 pounds. When I got up the courage to sign up for basketball tryouts, I knew it would be an uphill battle. With not much surprise, after two days of the longest physical activity of my life, I didn't make the team. I was devastated at the time. One of my windows had closed…

This defeat made me think a lot of some of the challenges I had growing up with my therapies, always having to put in the time if I wanted to get the results. With that mantra in mind, I spent the rest of my freshman year getting myself in the best physical shape possible. I started working out five times a week, practicing my craft in basketball camps, and when sophomore year came, I was 60 pounds lighter and also 3 inches taller to boot.

I went into that year with the confidence and dedication needed to do what was necessary, and I made it. I made our junior varsity (JV) team sophomore year, and followed that up to make varsity junior year and varsity captain senior year. This mantra became something I was so proud of that I started to make this a way to look at everything I was doing in my life—putting in the effort to get the things I really cared about.

While basketball was critical, my other interest was in theater arts. Much like basketball, I started this knowing I wanted to go from watching people perform to becoming an actor. I decided to make acting part of my therapy to become better at communication. I took elements of social story therapy my mother had used for years, and turned it into performing in plays. Unlike basketball, though, I had started theater when I was five years old with mixed results, because I neither wanted to be with other kids in groups, nor could I handle the attention, while being on stage, of things like clapping, which made me tantrum and cry uncontrollably in the early years. Theater had always been a form of therapy for me, but I didn't focus on it as much until high school. I went from high school to being in two plays and the lead in my senior year. Because of theater the transition to college was easier because I had become more vocal and confident in my public speaking.

Because of these two interests, along with forming a great routine, I had a very successful high school experience, and was really looking forward to college. When I first started out in high school, the thought of college really never seemed possible due to my limitations. When junior year started, and I was taking the SATs I thought it would be even more impossible. Because of my communication issues early on, I have always struggled with comprehension, especially when it comes to reading and retaining information. Multiple-question tests have never been a strength for me. After countless review courses and trips to tutors in New York City and New Jersey, going into the SAT prep I still couldn't muster more than 420 on the verbal, but compensated in writing, and like many other Auties, great math scores, which left me with a decent combined 1540 on my SATs.

I was not thrilled with my scores at first. I kept thinking to myself that those scores wouldn't get me anywhere. Because of the stress I had during that time, I decided that I needed to apply EVERYWHERE. I had to get in somewhere, and that made me apply to 15 colleges, all on the East Coast (the farthest away was Syracuse University in Upper State New York). I applied to St. Peters College, New Jersey City University, Stevens Institute of Technology, Seton Hall University (SHU) in state, St. Thomas Aquinas, Syracuse University, and nine others. Luckily my parents were able to get many of those college application fees waived, and coming out of senior year I had 15 chances to see my goal of getting into college a reality.

When it came to these decisions, I knew I wanted to go somewhere where I could get a major in a business-related field to use my math. More than anything, I wanted to do something in the sports marketing field one day. It became easy enough to find colleges that had four-year business programs, not that many concentrations in sports management, but difficult to find places that had good disability support programs. My parents, who played a critical part in helping me with this process, were skeptical about some of the schools because of these limitations. I, being young and a little naïve, went in with the mentality that any school I went to would have been fine with supports. I thought, "I'm sure all these schools are becoming more disability-friendly."

When senior year began, I was a wreck. My nerves were all over the place. In one of the first weeks of that year I told my parents that I was even considering joining the Peace Corps after high school to avoid the disappointment of not getting in anywhere, not acknowledging they wouldn't want me without a college degree. My parents had more hope than I had for myself at the time. They told me to keep my head up and just see what happened. They thought I would get in somewhere.

Then the day came when the letters started making their way to the house. The first college I was heard from was St. Peter's

College in my hometown, with a $14,000 merit scholarship. It wasn't my top school but it was definitely one I would consider an option to attend. I remember there being a few minutes of hesitation before I opened it. When I finally came up with the courage somewhere deep inside me to open the letter, things became a little brighter...

I MADE IT INTO COLLEGE!!!

Oh what a rush it was to see my name on an acceptance letter! After all the concerns of not being smart enough, someone wanted me to attend their school! As we got closer to graduation day, the next 14 letters came slowly, but surely. When the last letter came in, my parents and I were stunned.

All 15 schools had accepted me! Not one rejection. The scholarships that came in combined counted for more than $150,000 too! I couldn't believe my luck. I now knew at least for the next four years where I would be, and that was in a place I had only dreamed of a few years earlier...

The university I decided to attend was based again on my interest in business and math. They even had a concentration in sports management, which put this university at the top.

In June 2007, I graduated from high school. It was an amazing time for me. The majority of my classmates and I were off to great new beginnings, at least on paper. "This is going to be great!" I thought to myself on many occasions that summer, before the first day of classes. (Later someone would point out to me the indicator for tracking disabled students should not be how many make it in, but how many make it out of, college.)

Fifteen years later, after my initial diagnosis, where everything seemed very uncertain, I was now heading to SHU in South Orange, New Jersey. I had one important stop to make during the summer between high school and college. I won a scholarship from the Autism Society of America and got to go to Scottsdale, Arizona, for a conference, where I won the CVS All Kids Can award. I was on my way. It must be great to be autistic; after all, I won a national award for it. Right? Maybe.

So I've gone into some detail here, discussing my earlier days before college. Now, if I had to pick a name for my college story, it would be titled "Dude! Where's my IEP?"—for all the preparation I had when first starting at Seton Hall, no one had ever indicated to me that my Individualized Education Program (IEP) was going to go away. Though I had sat in on my IEPs in high school, it was something that was never brought up to me. It made for a very awkward situation.

This led me to develop the prime directive for every student who goes to college with a disability—if you want to help others in a college setting, you have to first learn to advocate for yourself, and in doing so, learn the nuts and bolts of your disability, and how it impacts learning, so that you can advocate to help others do the same. A tall order for a 19-year-old kid.

Before this day happened, however, all new incoming freshmen had to attend a summer "orientation period." During this period we would have the chance to spend the night in freshman dorms, receive our laptops, and also get to meet several faculty members at the school. In addition to this, I had one additional separate meeting that most of the other freshmen didn't—an accommodation meeting with the director of disability support services at SHU. This is when the ball dropped for me.

I was going in for an orientation day at SHU and had set up a meeting with the director of our disability support services. The conversation started with a discussion of accommodations I had received in high school, and what I thought I needed for college. That was when the bomb hit me. IEPs no longer existed, and under Section 504, "reasonable accommodations" had been put in its place. Talk about a complete 180! My biggest thought going through my head was, "Oh, this is the same thing because the accommodations I got in my IEP seemed reasonable enough." Oh how wrong I was at that moment...

During the meeting I learned many intriguing and frightening things about how college was going to be a huge difference from high school; the main difference for me was going to be "the IEP," that *I would not have one.* I can't believe I was that oblivious that this was going to happen. Later, I learned that under the Individuals with Disabilities Education Act (IDEA), the IEP only exists from kindergarten to twelfth grade. At the college door you get a Section 504 accommodations plan, which is a Civil Rights Act, and if you have a physical disability, an American with Disabilities Act (ADA) accommodation.

In college, there are only "reasonable accommodations" to help make the classes accessible to those specific students with disabilities. The bottom line: there is no plan for you. Your professors don't even know you are entitled to accommodations unless you tell them, and then it's more of a negotiation with each professor as to how it gets implemented. Some professors are great and helpful, and some not so much (sort of like life!). The only way to receive what you need is by being independent and advocating for your needs. But what does anyone need? If you are a freshman and have autism and a communication disorder, how do you know how much, let alone explain what you need? And how many students want to admit they are disabled to begin with? I will tell you how many students at that door will not choose to seek accommodations to their total detriment. I have had friends with disabilities, away for the first time from their home and support systems, who find themselves isolated in the wrong setting, and are so overwhelmed to the point that they have a breakdown, and many were forced to drop out when they really could have made it with support from their parents, who got them to this point. Disability services rely on tough love to make the student responsible since you are now an adult, but the pulling out of parental involvement in an effort to make them self-sufficient is simply something most students entering college are not prepared for. There needs to be true transition services between high school and college if students are going to have a chance to succeed. And looking back, it probably has to start in middle school.

At times, for me this led to many distractions that never would have occurred when I was younger. Sometimes I thought it was unfair. I had to advocate for my own single room in the dorms due to my social complications. I wound up making up a fictional roommate who had appendicitis to tell my roommates the reason why I was a single student in a double room. On paper it said I had extended time on tests due to my deficits in reading comprehension, a note-taker for my classes due to auditory processing deficits and dysgraphia (lack of motor skills), and many other complications like taking the exam itself. Now who actually sets this stuff up for you? Disability services staffed with a few staff members will help to some extent, but the bottom line is, it falls on you. A huge shock. In class, finding someone to give the test to you with extended time was a challenge, and my favorite—student couriers losing the exams in the process of it being carted back and forth between the professor and disability services offices—or my all-time worst—the professor sending it by computer to disability services and them not being able to open the file. (Test anxiety and stress, anyone?) And I learned early on that although taping my classes worked best for me, that was not a given. Professors often own their coursework as their intellectual property, and it is totally within their discretion to deny you the right to audiotape. I, in my junior and senior years, prepared and signed a non-disclosure form to promise not to distribute the tape beyond my needed use.

For someone trying to fit in, it seemed like it was designed to make you stand out like a sore thumb. It even seemed as if as soon as I accomplished one of these tasks, the next semester would begin, and it would start all over again for my new courses, which required different accommodations.

Timing was also a real issue. We needed our accommodations meeting at the disability support services to occur in the first two weeks after classes began at the start of each semester, the theory being you should experience the class before you went to support services. But disability support services got us scheduled long after the add/drop transfer period was over.

I'm for a class/professor matching. Despite my being in a leadership honors program, an elite program for 15 freshmen, in my non-honors classes I found myself matched up with teachers who required quizzes every class—as I was entitled to extended time, guess how that worked out? Not in my favor, I assure you—the logistics of the class and the annoyance of the teacher to provide the accommodation every class just made me give up the accommodation. In my freshman year one of my teachers didn't want me to use my computer for tests, and he actually said my handwritten answers looked like the scribble of a three-year-old. Guess I made up the dysgraphia diagnosis, then. Which means I can't hold a writing instrument without great difficulty, which is why I normally type everything. (AND VERY WELL.) And my auditory processing disorder took my classes to a new dimension, which led to someone actually listening to my tapes in the beginning so I could sort out whether I had heard the directions for the course.

All of this is in hindsight, and should be used for planning courses for disabled students; I strongly recommend a peer mentoring program for disabled students, and keeping some sort of book to familiarize students with what will be expected from teachers in classes, so you can choose the sections of class that you might actually have a chance in and that fit your learning style. Now that would be a reasonable accommodation for sure.

When you add this to managing a full course load, trying to socialize with your fellow peers, along with being involved in extra-curricular activities, it felt at times like I was drowning. I mean, "reasonable accommodations" are supposed to help level the playing field, not hinder you in any way. There isn't a "reasonable accommodation" for that.

Although getting accommodations was sometimes daunting, I was still able to get by after trial and error, and actually some of the gimmicks, like note-talking and a good scheduler of my 24-hour day, helped a lot. I had the Community School advantage of having a scheduler with me at all times. For several semesters I sat up front and taped most of my classes and downloaded the recordings onto my computer, instead of utilizing a note-taker. Never would have thought of that in my freshman year. For those reading this who are younger and not yet in college, my advice is to sit in on as many IEP meetings with your parents in high school as you can. Learn and ask as many questions as possible. The letters after your diagnosis don't tell you if you need extended time or a note-taker, but knowing if you are a visual or auditory learner may. For as much preparation as I had, my mother kept an index card of where I was supposed to be the first day of each semester, because I invariably called and asked her semester in and semester out on that first day where my classes were located—for four straight years I called her on the first day to ask if she knew where I was supposed to be. Transitions are just difficult for me.

Also make use of tutors. There are tutors for everything at college, You don't need to be disabled, there are tutors in almost every dorm—find the schedule and use them as well as the writing centers that actually will help you rewrite your papers, if you don't wait till the last minute. Knowing you have someone to lean on to help get you through will make an enormous difference, especially in freshman year. Some schools have disabled programs where freshmen actually check in every week to make sure you don't fall behind. Mine didn't, but it is a good idea. Learning what technology programs you can use as an aide before you start school is another good one, as well as the decision to buy online or hard-copy books. Or both. Some online books come with printable note cards that can be an aide for review.

Within this I would also strongly consider letting your parents be involved in some of your early decision-making, especially when it includes freshman year accommodations. Independence is not grown over night, and we all need that added voice sometimes to make sure we are level headed and know exactly what we are getting ourselves into. Also, if you are sitting in a college disability support services office, you must have had tremendous support from your parents, so don't cut the cord too abruptly, as even though the office don't want them there, they are probably still writing the checks for your tuition. Make disability support services find a balance.

As many say, early intervention is the key once first diagnosed—early intervention for those on the spectrum in college (and high school and probably middle school for that matter as well) is the key to ultimate success. What I've noticed about autism over the years is that it's not a weakness unless you let it become one. Don't let it hinder you. Let the advantages of who you are and what you have to offer be your ability to make it at college level; just always know what your weaknesses are so you can be ready for whatever is to come next!

An unexpected negative consequence for me was, as a disabled student, in the beginning I was limited to 12 credits, but I paid tuition based on a semester charge that would have allowed me to take 18 credits. I then had to pay $6000 extra for summer classes to stay on track to graduate with my class—doesn't seem fair, does it? Eventually I took some summer classes at state schools to lighten the financial burden, but again, some classes have to be taken at your home college, and this requires planning.

Because of all of the reactions I had, especially in the orientation period and my first few weeks at school, I wanted to make a conscious effort to advocate for myself. During my oral communication class we had an assignment to pick a subject we were passionate about, and then give a 15-minute presentation on it. For me, the topic I had in mind came right away. My topic was focused on autism awareness. As the day of the presentation came, I kept playing around with my PowerPoint slides, and trying to find ways to make it more dynamic. One suggestion that came from a tutor I had for the course was to end off with a powerful closing statement.

I kept thinking to myself what would a powerful closing statement even look like, and then it hit me. I was going to mention that I was on the autism spectrum. This was something I was originally thinking about doing within the first week of classes, but really had no idea how to bring it up without it seeming random. So, the day of the presentation came, and I was admittedly a bit of a nervous wreck about presenting. When it was finally my turn to go up to the podium and speak, though, everything just seemed to click. The first 10 minutes or so clicked because I was just talking about what I already knew about autism. Then, as the last 5 minutes started, I become more nervous as I knew my closing statement was coming. I slowed down my pace by a great margin, and then I paused. I was panicking in my head. No words wanted to come out.

It wasn't until I started to process the good this would do for me in my head that I continued and said my closing line, which was "I can relate to many people who I've talked about today as I also have autism. The main thing to remember about autism is that even though it's a disability, it can't define who we are. Only we can define autism. Thank you for listening to my presentation today."

After that I picked up my papers and was beginning to walk to my seat when I was greeted with thunderous applause by my peers, with smiles all about. I felt so emotional at the time I had almost begun to cry. I had no idea how anyone would react to a presentation like that, and I had ended up with that. It truly made an impact that has stayed with me after all these years of advocacy work. The next year I had taken my advocacy work to another level on my college campus by starting the first ever organization on our campus to spread disability awareness, called the Student Abilities Association (later know as Student Disability Awareness). Its primary goals were to reach out, connect, and support SHU students who have disabilities that are either temporary or permanent. We became an informational resource on campus for SHU's students with disabilities; you did not have to have a disability to join, and soon many kids were participating in awareness-raising activities (walks, fundraising, and volunteerism) to increase knowledge of issues relating to disability. We were used as a resource by the administration to help eliminate barriers of any type (e.g. physical, programmatic, attitudinal, or electronic), and we encouraged personal growth and increasing effective communication for students with disabilities. I am happy to report that six years later, the group is still functioning on Seton Hall's campus. Now that is making an impact that I can be proud of—that I helped other students come to a place where a support group is in place that I didn't have when I arrived on campus. It made me a student leader on campus, and led me to do something that, looking back, might have been crazy. At the end of my freshman year I applied to be a resident advisor (RA) in the dorms. One of my primary reasons is because as an RA, I would get my own single room. So, for the next two years, I was, as a disabled autistic student, responsible for the care of 99 students, first in Neumann Hall, and then Aquinas. I gave it up in the second semester of junior year because I had to take my off-campus internship at CBS Sports NYC. The time doing this, though, was completely surreal to me. Being a role model for my peers gave me a great feeling.

I had a few run-ins with the authorities both directly and indirectly while I was away at college. Many of them occurred due to circumstances that were out of my control, and some I could have prepared for better. There were many incidents I was shaken by during the time when I was in school and in my internship. The first incident happened in freshman year when I had just moved into dorms. I was living with two suitemates, but had my own disability single room attached to the suite. One day, in the morning, around 6am, I heard loud bangs on our suite door. I woke up startled, and the next thing I heard someone scream, "Open up! It's the police!" This was followed up by four or five more loud bangs on the door while I, scared out of my mind, just buried my head in my pillow with anxiety.

After a few seconds of silence, one of my suitemates opened the door and the police said they needed to talk about an incident that had happened at a college party involving an assault accusation. While I heard the conversation go back and forth, I just stayed quiet, while listening to the dialogue. A few minutes later they left with my suitemate, and I, out of exhaustion and a bit of fear, passed out, right back to bed.

A few weeks later everything went back to normal. I never found out what happened or if the incident had led to any legal actions, but my suitemates were still there, so I imagined everything had gone away. Everything seemed to slow down until another incident shook our campus with a campus lockdown involving a gun accusation later that year. Someone who had been shot had apparently made it past our gates and had dropped his weapon somewhere on campus. I remember being at our school newspaper meeting when they told us we weren't allowed to leave the building. Rumors started spreading like wildfire. Some people had said several students were killed, while others said that it was just a prank by some immature students. By the time we were let out a few hours later I remember being extremely terrified leaving the building. When I mustered the courage to leave, the first thing I saw overhead was a helicopter circling our campus with bright lights flashing all over. I instinctively ran back to my dorm, opened the door to my suite, locked it, and put my head in my pillow again, passing out right away as I had a midterm in business ethics the next morning. No one checked in on me. The next year I became the first autistic RA on SHU campus, and believe me, I checked on my residents in all situations.

I didn't have another incident with the authorities until I moved off-campus. I, and my roommate, went to a local store a block away from our apartment. On our way back these two guys, probably in their late 20s, approached us. They approached us rather quickly, and one of them said, "Police. What do we have here?" pointing at our bags. The next thing I know they are asking for our IDs, with me shaking for all hell. The officer said, "Excuse me. Why do you look so nervous?" I responded back honestly, "This is a scary situation."

After both cops saw that I and my roommate were over the age of 21, they both said we were free to go. I was a mess after this! From a sensory standpoint I was so stressed by having strangers come up and interrogate me and my friend. A few months later I was also pulled over at around midnight for an issue with my high beams. When the officer asked for my registration, I realized that my father, whose car I was driving, had never updated it. My dad's car was towed away 30 minutes later, and I was stranded off-campus with my friend. Overall, these experiences of dealing with authorities have been very unpleasant but have also been eye-opening to me, as I realize that some circumstances will always be out of your control. Not everything can be planned out all the way. Sometimes you will just have to roll with the punches and hope for the best, and a note to myself that, although I carry a disabled residents ID for my handicapped car sticker, I have never told a police authority in these situations that I am disabled. Whether that would have made things go smoother I'll never know.

The last incident was when I started my internship in New York City. I had never taken a bus alone before starting college. Now, in the middle of the winter, I was taking the school shuttle to the train station from suburban South Orange, a train into New York City, and then getting to CBS headquarters on 11th Avenue. One of my first encounters with the authorities was a police officer screaming at me because I jaywalked, obliviously, with my headphones, across 7th Avenue. I'm sure he was trying to save my life, but at the time, I was frightened to death, and definitely would caution anyone reading this who has not started college to run through the scenarios of what to do when stopped by the authorities.

I also know I had to give up or modify my dreams along the way. I had always assumed that I would go to law school to become a sports agent. And the reality is despite graduating with departmental honors at Stillman School of Business, I was cautioned that although I would probably get through the rigorous academic work, I would probably never pass the bar exam because the nature of the professional licensing exams don't lend themselves to accommodations. With that in the back of my mind, I applied to not one law school, not even to see if I could get in.

After my four years at Seton Hall, going through all the tribulations with accommodations, I decided to go back for my Master's in strategic communications and leadership. Ever since those first few weeks when I knew I wanted to do work in self-advocacy, I became hooked on trying to help others. This made getting a Master's an easy decision for me. I wanted to now get the education needed to take my self-advocacy work out of Seton Hall to the rest of the world.

The major difference between my undergraduate and graduate path was that when I was getting my Master's, I decided not to use any of my accommodations. I didn't even present any letters to my teachers. The Master's program has been simplified a great deal because of more online courses and more one-on-one training. Most of the things I would need from accommodations, like a note-taker and tests, had been eliminated. Most of the work involved writing papers and group projects. One of my biggest projects was working on my Master's thesis, which ended up being over 50 pages long. I was now going into a field where I was more comfortable, and it led to me graduating with a 3.96 GPA in only a year-and-a-half!

The rest I can say has been gravy to this point. Shortly after graduating, I started working full-time in digital media close to home, along with continuing my work around the country as a national motivational speaker. My first book, *Defining Autism from the Heart*, came out, and I am still hanging onto my goal of spreading autism education to the world by contributing to 30 books by the time I turn 30 in 2018 (no pressure, right?).

At around the same time I started Student Disability Awareness during my sophomore year of college, I also began working on a plan for after college. With the same basis for trying to help those with disabilities, I started the organization KFM Making a Difference, focused on providing affordable housing and scholarships for those with special needs. Two years after I filled out the paperwork to form the organization, I began talking with the IRS to make it non-profit. In 2013, after almost a year-and-a-half of waiting, I got the final confirmation that it had been granted public non-profit status.

I can now say today that I founded and own a non-profit. Since the non-profit came about, we have worked in New Jersey on best practice towards our long-term goal of starting special needs housing for young adults in transition. As part of our shorter-term goals, though, we've been able to start our scholarship program called Making a Difference for Autism. We have given out a scholarship each academic semester since it started in the Fall 2012 to aspiring college students who are also on the autism spectrum. I've personally been blown away by how many gifted individuals we have out there within our community. When I applied to college, I only found one or two scholarships for those on the autism spectrum. I often wondered why that was so. I now know exactly why: no one believed that students with autism could go on to college. I proved them wrong, and through my fundraising efforts, I hope my scholarship signifies the beginning of breaking down that barrier for my community—we are capable of doing amazing things.

One of the more rewarding parts of doing what I do now in speaking is I get to share some of my experiences with younger individuals on the spectrum who are first starting out in high school and college. This was something I sorely missed when I was first starting off. I always wanted a role model who I could look up to who was going through similar experiences that I was. Even growing up I didn't really have that many peers that I knew of who were on the autism spectrum.

I can honestly say looking back now, that going to college was well worth the time and one of the best experiences of my life. My biggest regret though may have been not spending enough time looking at disability support programs while looking at colleges. The silver lining to all of this, though, was my support team at home in my mom and dad. Just like they were there to help me with my college applications, they stood by me through thick and thin in college, and were something like coaches to keep me focused on what I needed to do.

Changes that I would make start with an awareness and education plan put in for all post-secondary programs. Those with special needs are already at a disadvantage compared to their peers because they have to do more just to get the chance to succeed. From a national level, with the discussion of bills like the Combating Autism Reauthorization Act, and now the proposed AGE-IN bill sponsored by Senator Robert Menendez focusing on adults in transition, it would be a nice change of pace to see these types of bills looking at those with special needs transitioning to these programs. Scholarships can be made from a federal level to encourage additional programs to help support services for those with disabilities. Wouldn't that be wonderful!

Above all else, though, I want people to know that autism can't define anyone with autism. These individuals define autism. They are gifted and brilliant individuals who have overcome many obstacles to make it to this point, and deserve the acceptance of their peers and their communities. I know so many gifted young people out there today, and with the right opportunities, they will have a chance to succeed. It's something our community definitely deserves, and I hope they are given every chance for that.

13

Conclusion

Building Inclusive Campuses

Pavan John Antony and Stephen M. Shore

The stories shared in the different chapters of this book attest to the fact that disability is not a barrier for many individuals to pursue or earn a college education in the United States. Like other typically developing students, individuals with disabilities will face challenges during their college education. These challenges can vary greatly between students and from campus to campus. They can vary from physical accessibility to lack of accommodation in the classroom and social challenges such as being bullied. The students could have both positive and negative experiences while attending college, interacting with fellow students, professionals, and community members on and off campus.

For example, a student with cerebral palsy highlighted in one of the chapters shared that it took him more than 16 years to earn his Bachelor's degree. Students with autism commonly reported difficulties in social interaction with their classmates, professors, and others, on and off campus. The story of the student with an intellectual disability portrayed in the book who initially doubted his ability to pursue college completed his education, and shared that it was a wonderful experience. Similarly, students with attention deficit hyperactivity disorder (ADHD) and a learning disability shared their ongoing challenges while attending college. However, they succeeded in earning their degrees. Similarly, the motivation to become a developmental psychologist encouraged a student with multiple disabilities, including autism and post-traumatic stress disorder (PTSD), to complete her undergraduate and graduate education.

The individuals portrayed in this book are real-life examples encouraging everyone to consider college as a viable option. Although research highlights the increasing enrollment of youth with disabilities in post-secondary programs, there remains a lack of inquiry into the daily experiences of individuals who continue their education and who enter the community. The daily experiences and the life after college education of the individuals highlighted in this book provide an opportunity for readers to understand higher education for individuals with disabilities.

Students with disabilities enrolling in colleges in the USA have increased dramatically during the past few decades. Even as early as the academic year 2008–09, "88 percent of 2-year and 4-year Title IV degree granting postsecondary institutions reported enrolling students with disabilities" (Raue and Lewis 2011, p.3), with public institutions nearing 100 percent for both two- and four-year colleges (Raue and Lewis 2011). This report also highlighted the fact that 86 percent of students had specific learning disabilities, while 79 percent had ADHD. It was also reported that 76 percent of students had physical disabilities, and 76 percent mental illness/psychological or psychiatric conditions (Raue and Lewis 2011). Research also highlights that 60 percent of students with disabilities attending post-secondary institutions are in community colleges (Ankeny and Lehmann 2010). These facts regarding the increased numbers of students with disabilities enrolling in colleges provides evidence for educators, parents, professionals, and individuals with disabilities to consider higher education as a viable option after graduating from high school. It is extremely important that transition specialists and teachers work closely with students with disabilities and their parents or guardians to develop individualized transition plans. These person-centered plans should be developed as a team, and should include continuing education into adulthood as appropriate to the individual.

The need for careful planning to develop individualized transition plans helping youth with disabilities transition to adulthood was affirmed in 1990 with the Individuals with Education Act, reauthorized in 1997 and 2004. However, despite these legal requirements, students with disabilities continue to face significant challenges after graduating from high school, such as employment, independent living, achieving financial independence, and community involvement (Kellems and Morningstar 2010; Kohler and Greene 2004). Lack of higher education on graduating from college could be one of the factors that leads to these kinds of challenges for many individuals with disabilities. It is important to acknowledge the benefits of a college degree for any individual upon graduating from high school. For example, a person with a college degree is almost always at an advantage for getting a job compared to a person without any post-secondary education. Wehman and Yasuda (2005) have already highlighted the benefits of having a college degree—higher earnings, benefits, career advancement, status, and marketability. They have also highlighted the invaluable experiences a student can obtain by attending a good college. College education can also help students with disabilities to improve their skills in reading, writing, planning, organizing, thinking, socializing, networking, and securing jobs (Wehman and Yasuda 2005). Despite these benefits, individuals with disabilities still face challenges beyond their peers who don't have disabilities in finding meaningful employment. This is evident in some of the chapters where authors, despite being highly qualified, have shared their continuing challenge to secure jobs due to their disability.

According to the US Department of Education, much of the challenge in achieving success in higher education focuses on finding ways for individuals with disabilities to use their strengths. Today, as increasing numbers of individuals with disabilities are enrolling in programs in higher education institutions, the following checklist can be used as a guide for promoting success.

Checklist for promoting student success
High school

» Educate the student regarding the differences between high school and college:

  › academically

  › socially

  › campus geography.

» Become familiar with the general layout of the campus as well as navigating from one location to another.

» Obtain and keep records of existing accommodations.

» Parents, teachers, and other specialists should work together with the student to develop individualized transition plans incorporating higher education as an option for the student as appropriate to their ability.

» Help students to make informed decisions regarding their future educational plans upon graduating from high school.

» Encourage students to create a vision plan for post-secondary education (if appropriate) and learning strategies to succeed, face challenges, and deal with day-to-day issues or risks in college.

» Adopt an interview process as early as age 13 to help the student successfully transition from high school to higher education (Kellems and Morningstar 2010).

» Prepare students for college through...

  › completing applications

  › assembling related material

  › conducting mock interviews

  › creating mock college classroom environments and lectures.

» Involve family as equal partners in the planning process.

» Collaborate with local educational institutions during the planning phase.

» Host one-day conference-type events for high school juniors and seniors as well as their parents that highlight higher education opportunities for all learners (Kato, Nulty, and Olszewski 2006).

» Visit potential higher education institutions in local communities:

  › walk about their campus

  › sit in on classes (with prior permission)

  › take a tour of the library, dorm, and other facilities (keep accessibility in mind)

  › visit the disabilities office (sometimes referred to as the office of student success or other titles).

» Understand the college climate, program philosophy, academic adjustment, waivers and substitutions, course load, and expectations (Getzel 2005).

» Visit online resources such as www.thinkcollege.net.

» Organize a transition group that meets frequently (Kellems and Morningstar 2010).

» Invite speakers with disabilities to the high school who are currently enrolled in a college program, or those who have successfully completed their college education.

» Prepare students academically (Garrison-Wade and Lehmann 2009) and socially for success in higher education.

Choosing a college

» Some variables to consider when selecting possible institutions of higher education include:

› desired areas of study

› size of the department(s) of interest

› campus environment (urban, suburban, or rural)

› size of the campus

› living accommodation (dorms)

› class size

› distance from home

› accessibility (physical, educational, social-emotional).

» Ideally tour a single campus per day and take notes for your reference:

› meet with current students with and without disabilities

› meet with professors from your areas of interest

› visit possible accommodations in and off campus

› visit dining halls and lounge areas

› visit classrooms and libraries

› seek prior permission to sit in a college classroom in action.

» Visit the disabilities office to determine the following:

› existing disability support services

› their knowledge of your specific type of disability

› their willingness to learn about your disability as needed

› learning about your rights

> › requirements for obtaining accommodations and any deadlines that must be met

> › understanding the steps involved in receiving accommodation

> › learning about the necessary paperwork to complete the application process.

In college

GETTING ORIENTED

» Attend all orientations.

» Learn the layout of the campus, how to get between locations, and how long that takes.

» Learn the community.

» Meet with your advisor to plan for the semester.

» Work closely with disabilities office support personnel (if needed).

GETTING READY FOR YOUR COURSEWORK

» Register for classes (obtain assistance from your advisor if needed).

» Visit all your classes (if needed) prior to the first day of class.

» Meet with all professors (if needed) after the first class to share about any accommodations.

» Share your disability and how it affects your learning with your professor, if needed.

» Carefully review the syllabus.

» If you have field visits for your classes, meet with the placement office for accommodations.

» Determine the time needed to get to each of your classes from the place you stay (do not be late to your class).

Campus life

» Identify clubs or organizations of interest.

» Have a plan for self-monitoring of progress in courses.

» Identify academic and other resources on and off campus:

› writing center

› tutoring center

› health center

› recreation center

› community resource—shopping/dining/etc.

» Keep a map handy.

» Generate a checklist of resources that you may need regularly, e.g. parking, accessibility, emergency contacts/ services (sign up for emergency alert notices), related web resources, important phone numbers, emails, and addresses.

» Use a paper or electronic planner to plan ahead for each week.

» Learn about the expectations for each course that you are enrolled in during the semester.

» Organize your semester carefully by balancing your workload and other activities.

» Share your challenges or struggles related to your college education with your support people.

» Identify appropriate support people with whom you can share at the beginning of the semester. This could vary for each student. It could be a professor, mentor, or at times, the school counselor or disability support staff. The key is to find the right person(s).

» Consider doing a self-evaluation with the help of another professional (if needed) regarding your performance in college after the initial weeks in college, in the middle, and by the end of the semester.

Web resources

Transition Coalition, providing online information, support and professional development on topics related to the transition from school to adult life for youths with disabilities: www.transitioncoalition.org

National Longitudinal Transition Study 2, funded by the US Department of Education, documenting the experiences of a national sample of students aged 13–16 in 2000 as they moved from secondary school into adult roles: www.nlts2.org

National Secondary Transition Technical Assistance Center, What Works Transition Research Synthesis Project: www.nsttac.org/ebp/what_works

National Secondary Transition Technical Assistance Center, Evidence-based Secondary Transition Practices: www.nsttac.org/ebp/evidence_based_practice.aspx

Casey Life Skills, Online Assessment for Independent Living Skills, is a free practice tool and framework for working with youth in foster care. It assesses independent living skills and provides results instantly: www.caseylifeskills.org

Association on Higher Education and Disability (AHEAD), the premiere professional association committed to the full participation of those with disabilities in post-secondary education: www.ahead.org

Section 504 of the Rehabilitation Act of 1973, Discrimination based on disability, understanding your rights and responsibilities: www2.ed.gov/about/offices/list/ocr/publications.html#Section504

National Center on Secondary Education and Transition, coordinates national resources, offers technical assistance, and disseminates information related to secondary education and transition for young people with disabilities in order to create opportunities for them to achieve successful futures: www.ncset.org

Advancing science, serving society, a resource for students with disabilities majoring in science and technology: www.entrypoint.org

Career Opportunities for Students with Disabilities (COSD), a consortium to hire people with disabilities: http://cosdonline.org/

Disabilities, Opportunities, Internetworking, and Technology (DO-IT), resources to survive college: www.washington.edu/doit

LD online, resources for students with learning disabilities: www.ldonline.org

Think College! College Options for People with Intellectual Disabilities: www.thinkcollege.net/

Asperger/Autism Network works with individuals, families, and professionals to help people with Asperger's syndrome and similar autism spectrum profiles build meaningful, connected lives: www.aane.org

Asperger Syndrome and High Functioning Autism Association: www.ahany.org

United States Autism & Asperger Association, a non-profit organization that boasts a proud network of world-renowned professionals with expertise in autism, Asperger syndrome, and other related disorders: www.usautism.org

References

Ankeny, E. and Lehmann, J. (2010) "The transition lynchpin: The voices of individuals with disabilities who attended a community college transition program." *Community College Journal of Research and Practice 34*, 477–496.

Garrison-Wade, D.D. and Lehmann, J.P. (2009) "A conceptual framework for understanding students' with disabilities transition to community college." *Community College Journal of Research & Practice 33*, 5, 417–445.

Getzel, E.E. (2005) "Preparing for college." In E.E. Getzel and P. Wehman (eds) *Going to College: Expanding Opportunities for People with Disabilities* (pp.3–23). Baltimore, MD: Paul H. Brookes Publishing Co.

Kato, M.M., Nulty, B., and Olszewski, B.T. (2006) "Postsecondary academies." *Teaching Exceptional Children 39*, 1, 18–23.

Kellems, R. and Morningstar, M. (2010) "Tips for transition. Teaching exceptional children." *Council for Exceptional Children 43*, 2, 60–68.

Kohler, P. and Greene, G. (2004) "Strategies for integrating transition-related competencies into teacher education." *Teacher Education and Special Education 27*, 2, 146–162.

Raue, K. and Lewis, L. (2011) *Students with Disabilities at Degree-granting Postsecondary Institutions.* Washington, DC: US Department of Education, National Center for Education Statistics, US Government Printing Office.

Wehman, P. and Yasuda, S. (2005) "The need and the challenges associated with going to college." In E.E. Getzel and P. Wehman (eds) *Going to College: Expanding Opportunities for People with Disabilities* (pp.3–23). Baltimore, MD: Paul H. Brookes Publishing Co.

Subject Index

Author Index

Succeeding as a Student in the STEM Fields with an Invisible Disability

A College Handbook for Science, Technology, Engineering, and Math Students with Autism, ADD, Affective Disorders, or Learning Difficulties and their Families

Christy Oslund

Paperback: £14.99 / $24.95
ISBN: 978 1 84905 947 3
160 pages

The STEM fields (Science, Technology, Engineering and Math) attract many students with autism, ADD, affective disorders and related invisible disabilities who are highly intelligent and analytical, but who, upon entering higher education, may find that they struggle with independent living and a different way of learning.

This is a preparation guide for students and their families that explains everything they need to know about the university experience including classroom behavior, study skills, self-reliance, accessing support services, and when parents should and shouldn't get involved. Offering practical advice and strategies, this is a useful handbook that students can refer to again and again throughout their college years guiding them on their paths to becoming the inventors, scientists, engineers, and computer entrepreneurs of the future.

Christy Oslund is Co-ordinator of Student Disability Services in the Dean of the Students' Office at Michigan Technological University. She has a PhD in Rhetoric and Technical Communication from Michigan Technological University and an MA in Philosophy from Michigan State University. She is an active member of the Association on Higher Education and Disability (AHEAD).

Succeeding in College with Asperger Syndrome

A Student Guide

*John Harpur, Maria Lawlor
and Michael Fitzgerald*

Paperback: £14.99 / $22.95
ISBN: 978 1 84310 201 4
272 pages

College life is particularly stressful for students with Asperger Syndrome (AS) and the resources that colleges provide for such students are often inadequate. This much needed guide provides information to help these students prepare successfully for the rites and rituals of studying, interact with staff and fellow students, cope with expectations and pressures, and understand their academic and domestic responsibilities. How will I cope with the workload? What do I do if I feel ill? How do I make friends and initiate relationships with the opposite sex? Drawing on first hand interviews with AS students and direct clinical experience, the authors address these and many other questions thoughtfully and thoroughly, making practical recommendations.

Succeeding in College with Asperger Syndrome demystifies the range of college experiences for students with AS. It is a must for these students, their parents and counsellors alike, providing benefits that will continue throughout the college years and beyond.

John Harpur was a lecturer in the Department of Computer Science at the National University of Ireland, Maynooth. His research included a multidisciplinary project on Emotional Intelligence and Asperger Syndrome. Maria Lawlor is a consultant child and adolescent psychiatrist at the Child and Family Centre, St. Mary's Hospital, Drogheda, and lecturer in the Department of Psychiatry, Trinity College, Dublin. Michael Fitzgerald is the Henry Marsh Professor of child and adolescent psychiatry at the Child and Family Centre at Trinity College, Dublin.

A Freshman Survival Guide for College Students with Autism Spectrum Disorders

The Stuff Nobody Tells You About!

Haley Moss

Paperback: £14.99 / $19.95

ISBN: 978 1 84905 984 8

160 pages

How do you know which college is right for you? What happens if you don't get on with your roommate? And what on earth is the Greek system all about? As a university student with High-Functioning Autism, Haley Moss offers essential tips and advice in this insider's guide to surviving the Freshman year of college.

Chatty, honest and full of really useful information, Haley's first-hand account of the college experience covers everything students with Autism Spectrum Disorders need to know. She talks through getting ready for college, dorm life and living away from parents, what to expect from classes, professors and exams, and how to cope in new social situations and make friends.

This book is a must-read for all students on the autism spectrum who are about to begin their first year of college, parents and teachers who are helping them prepare, and college faculty and staff.

Haley Moss is a 19-year-old student with High-Functioning Autism. She has recently completed her Freshman year at University of Florida where she is pursuing a Bachelor of Science in Psychology and a Bachelor of Arts in Criminology. She is also taking a minor in Disabilities in Society. Haley is the author of Middle School: The Stuff Nobody Tells You About, she is a keen advocate for autism, and she is a frequent speaker at autism events. She has won numerous awards including a Hope for Children "Teen Hero Award." She is also a talented artist.

Helping Students with Autism Spectrum Disorder Express their Thoughts and Knowledge in Writing

Tips and Exercises for
Developing Writing Skills

Elise Geither and Lisa Meeks

Paperback: £16.99 / $26.95
ISBN: 978 1 84905 996 1
136 pages

When it comes to academic work, students with Autism Spectrum Disorder (ASD) often have the required knowledge but struggle to get their thoughts down in writing. This is a practical guide to teaching and improving writing skills in students with ASD to meet academic writing standards and prepare for the increased expectations of higher education.

The book covers key considerations for all educators teaching writing skills to high school and college students with ASD including how to address difficulties with comprehension, executive functioning, and motor skills, how to structure ideas into a coherent argument, and how to develop creativity and expression in writing, as well as how to successfully adapt these skills to meet university expectations. Each chapter includes teaching tips, insightful student perspectives, and ready-to-use writing exercises.

Elise Geither, PhD, is Associate Director of Spoken English Programs at Case Western Reserve University, Ohio. She has over 20 years of experience teaching, tutoring, and advising students at the university level and previously worked as an English teacher in secondary level education. She specializes in working with students with Autism Spectrum Disorder who are transitioning from high school to university. She lives in North Ridgeville, OH.

Lisa Meeks, PhD, is Director of Student Disability Services at the University of California, San Francisco. She has done extensive work in the area of transitions for students with Autism Spectrum Disorder developing specialized supports at three universities and she frequently consults with corporate and academic institutions regarding effective supports for students on the spectrum. She lives in San Francisco, CA.